Praise

Yvonne Orji and *Ba*

"Inspiration practically leaps off the pages and into the hearts of readers—the writing is engaging and the comedic timing is absolute gold. Orji is a cheerleader and best friend for every dreamer."

—*Booklist*

"Not only is Yvonne really funny and smart, she brings a fresh new perspective to every story she tells. She is an absolute master, and an original voice that needs to be heard now more than ever. Once you let her in your mind, you'll never want her to leave."

—Chris Rock, actor and comedian

"Yvonne somehow found a way to brilliantly weave her humor, insight, courage, and faith into pages that feel like a weekend retreat hanging with your best, boldest, brightest, and most blessed girlfriend. *Bamboozled by Jesus* is real talk about deep faith put in practice from a woman committed to living a life of vision, purpose, service, and success."   Kerry Washington, actress, producer, and director

"Whether it's as an actress, comedian, or thought-leader, Yvonne has always given a fresh perspective and authentic storytelling. *Bamboozled* is a culmination of the characteristics that make her so special: sharp wit, fierce intelligence, and an unapologetic sense of self."

—Rachel Hollis, author and speaker

"A delightful debut…Orji's boundless enthusiasm will appeal to her fans and newcomers alike."   —*Publishers Weekly*

BAMBOOZLED
by Jesus

HOW GOD TRICKED ME
INTO THE LIFE OF MY DREAMS

YVONNE ORJI

WORTHY
PUBLISHING

New York • Nashville

Worthy
Hachette Book Group
1290 Avenue of the Americas, New York, NY 10104
worthypublishing.com
twitter.com/worthypub

Originally published in hardcover and ebook by Worthy in May 2021

First trade paperback edition: September 2023

Worthy is a division of Hachette Book Group, Inc. The Worthy name and logo are trademarks of Hachette Book Group, Inc.

The publisher is not responsible for websites (or their content) that are not owned by the publisher.

The Hachette Speakers Bureau provides a wide range of authors for speaking events. To find out more, go to hachettespeakersbureau.com or email HachetteSpeakers@hbgusa.com.

Scripture quotations marked (NIV) are taken from the Holy Bible, New International Version®, NIV®. Copyright © 1973, 1978, 1984, 2011 by Biblica, Inc.™ Used by permission of Zondervan. All rights reserved worldwide. www.zondervan.com. The "NIV" and "New International Version" are trademarks registered in the United States Patent and Trademark Office by Biblica, Inc.™ | Scripture quotations marked (AMP) are taken from the Amplified® Bible, Copyright © 1954, 1958, 1962, 1964, 1965, 1987 by The Lockman Foundation. Used by permission. (www.Lockman.org) | Scripture quotations marked MSG are taken from The Message, copyright © 1993, 2002, 2018 by Eugene H. Peterson. Used by permission of NavPress, represented by Tyndale House Publishers. All rights reserved. | Scripture quotations marked KJV are from the King James Version of the Holy Bible.

Library of Congress Control Number: 2020952333

ISBNs: 978-1-5460-1267-2 (hardcover); 978-15460-1268-9 (trade paperback); 978-1-5460-1269-6 (ebook)

Printed in the United States of America

LSC-C

Printing 1, 2023

Hey, Boo.

Yes, you! In case you didn't know, someone you've never even met is counting on you. They're waiting on your "yes," to living your dreams out loud, so that they, too, can dream new dreams and believe in more than their circumstances dictate. No pressure, but…*pressure*. The weight of the world is *not* on your shoulders, but it should stir you up to know that your life is bigger than the family you were born into or the school you go to, the job you work at or the church you attend. Your sphere of influence is much larger, and God wants to highlight you to nations you don't e'en know about yet.

You're gonna be a change agent in your community. The one to break generational curses in your family and alter the legacy of your lineage. God has called, equipped, and empowered you to be *you*—exactly as you are. Think about it: The mother of the Savior was an unwed teenage girl. The second-in-command over Egypt was a former slave. The woman who saved her family from death and destruction was a prostitute. One of the greatest warriors in history was a forgotten shepherd boy. So why can't **YOU** do dope things? You can! That's the point. Even without the "right" connections, you're fine. Even though your funds are low, you'll make it. Even when your hope is fading, pick it back up, boo. It gets darkest before it gets the brightest. So, don't give up. Scratch that, I won't let you give up. The world is waiting on your supply. Get to it, fam!

y.O.

*To all the immigrant parents who sacrifice so much,
so their children can inherit the much more.
You arrive at distant shores filled with uncertainty,
resilience, and profound loss—of community, of
the life you imagined, of home. I am the daughter
of such immigrants. I am the answered prayers of
ancestors. I am because they did(n't).*

CONTENTS

IN THE BEGINNING...

I was born holding my mom's IUD (intrauterine device) in my hand.

True story.

After three sons, my parents decided that their baby-making days were over. Clearly, God was like, "nah." And nine months later, I defiantly bust outta the womb clutching the very device meant to prevent my conception.

That was my first taste of being bamboozled by Jesus.

I see the look of horror on the face of everyone either using, or contemplating using, an IUD. *Relaaaax.* That was in the '80s. In Nigeria. I'm sure there's been advances in medical technology by now. If not, just name the baby Godswill.

But ain't that just like God, tho? He's out here being the Sovereign Trickster in our lives, acting like the Ancient-of-Days Ashton Kutcher; running 'round town getting folks *Punk'd.* Personally, I've fallen for the bamboozlement of Jesus *several* times.

Like when I was a college freshman, and thought I was gonna live it up. I imagined my days consisting of partying, studying, partying some more—you know, the basics. Little did I know how quickly those plans would be kiboshed, and suddenly turned into: Attend a Bible study freshman year, commit my life to Jesus, and remain a virgin until I get married. What?! Who agreed to th—

Bamboozled.

Insert: TEDx Talk entitled "The Wait Is Sexy."

Oh, it didn't stop there.

After graduation, I planned on going to medical school—the pinnacle of success for every Nigerian child. Not according to Jesus, it wasn't. One day, out of left field, I heard Him tell me to perform stand-up comedy instead. *Well, that's just ridiculous*, I thought. I'd never done, nor desired to do, comedy, so I wouldn't even know the first thing abou—

Bamboozled.

Insert: HBO comedy special *Momma, I Made It!*

My life today is basically one big walking billboard of how God tricked me into living out my wildest dreams. I ain't madd at it, but along the way, I definitely had questions, and a few choice words for Jesus that didn't start with, "Dear Heavenly" anything! Thankfully, we made it, so like I said, I ain't madd at it.

Bamboozling people into a life they never could've imagined for themselves is kind of Jesus' m.o. All throughout the Bible, He's suckered several unsuspecting targets into a life full of prestige and promise. And by suckered, I mean dragged through struggle and pain before getting to the good stuff. But can you blame Jesus? He, *Himself*, got bamboozled. God told Him to come down to Earth, perform a few dope miracles ('cause who doesn't like a little wine at a party?)—but then set Him up for the okie-doke with the whole, die-on-a-cross-for-their-sins thing. Heck, even Jesus' own momma, Mary, got bamboozled when an angel rolled up on her like, *Hey, gurl, go'on ahead and have this here baby. Don't worry about the laws of biology or your boo-thang, Joseph. I got'chyu covered.*

Apparently, nobody's safe in these streetz. Errybody can get it.

Being bamboozled by Jesus is low-key, the most frustratingly amazing thing you'll ever experience. It ain't always sexy, but it is always worth it. But don't feel bad for wanting to tap out midway through. Even Jesus looked for an exit strategy. He straight up asked God, *If there be any other way, let this cup pass me by.* In other words, *Fam, this ain't it!* While you may want to chuck up the deuces, the only way out is to settle for less than God's best, and we're not about that life.

Before we go any further, I do want to put this disclaimer out there: You do not have to be a Bible scholar or devout evangelical to benefit from the pages in this book. I didn't go to anybody's seminary, nor am I an ordained anything. I'm just a young Black chick who entered into a beautiful relationship with a God I've never met, but who chose to love me in unimaginable ways. So if you don't subscribe to the whole "Christianity" thing, that's cool. Get in where you fit in. Personally, my faith impacts my success and my life in general, so it's hard for me to separate the two, but I promise to keep an open mind and heart, and all I ask is that you do the same. If it makes you feel any better, for every Bible story I tell, I'll throw in a DMX or Cardi B reference for good measure, 'cuz I'm well-rounded like that.

You're welcome.

> Being bamboozled by Jesus isn't always sexy, but it is always worth it.

Now, to all my Sunday school saints, you might as well go ahead and give me grace right now as you fact-check my biblical knowledge with your Judge Not Lest You Be Judged First New Living Word of Life First Baptist Church Special Edition Translation. I'm letting you know up front that I'm probably gonna do things that irk you, like referring to the Bible as Da Good Book, or DGB (*You down with DGB, yeah, you know me!*), or interchangeably using "Jesus" and "God," even though one is the Father and the other is the Son, but you know what? We're all gan'make it, so everybody calm down.

And before you push the blasphemy button, I am fully aware that some of the comparisons I make about your favorite Bible characters— like calling Abraham the first F-boy to ever exist—will elicit a sharp side-eye, and I'm okay with that. This is how Jesus and I get down. We've got our own thing going on, and He's the one who told me to be a comedian and write this book in the first place, so go ahead and take your complaints up with Management.

Now, if you're one of the folks thinking, *This book is ridiculous! Jesus is a loving Savior. He would never bamboozle anybody!* just ask yourself this one thing: Were you alive in 2020? If so, then you already know that entire year was one big bamboozled by Jesus petri dish. Errybody and their momma started off 2020 talkin'bout how it would be a season of clear focus and 20/20 vision. All the while, God sat back, gigglin' at us. We had no idea how glaringly clear things were about to become when, two and a half months into the year, the entire world shut down thanks to a pandemic called COVID-19 (or COVERED-19, depending on what clever spin your pastor put on it).

The coronavirus, and the subsequent global quarantine that followed, forced us all to get back to the basics of humanity, hope, and hygiene. My good friend Devi Brown described 2020 as a divine time-out. It was the best-worst kind of sit-down-and-face-the-wall that nobody asked for, but kinda desperately needed. We definitely could have done without the millions of deaths worldwide, the unprecedented unemployment rates, and the blatant racial injustice experienced in the United States. I'm also pretty certain that a few parents would've opted out of being teacher, breadwinner, *and* after-school entertainment all in one day and space.

BUUUT, 2020 did accomplish a few things. For starters, it exposed how fractured we are as a society, and offered opportunities for healing. It taught us how the busyness of our lives distracted us from dealing with ourselves. And ultimately, it solved the mystery of just how much toilet paper *is* enough for one household.

So yeah, nobody loves getting bamboozled, or twelve-plus months of incessant Zoom calls, but we do appreciate what we gain on the flip side. At least I do. That's why I bothered to write this book. To help you endure so you can *get* to the other side. Trust me, if getting bamboozled by Jesus only stopped at the sucky parts, then I'd be the first one telling you to exit stage left. But it doesn't. Hence the subtitle, *How God Tricked Me into the Life of My Dreams*.

Spoiler alert: Things worked out pretty well for me.

And I'm confident they'll work out great for you too! I'm not just saying that in a life-coachery kind of way. That's cute and all, but that ain't me. While I aim to be kind and understanding in these pages, I'm still an African immigrant woman at my core, and we have a limbo-low tolerance for excuses and self-imposed limitations. So if you were expecting cucumber sandwiches with a side of encouragement, please do us both a favor and regift this to your other, other best friend, 'cuz you got me twisted. I'm not the type of chick that'll give you advice like that friend you *love* to have. You know, the one who doesn't challenge you, who pacifies you, and allows you to lie to yourself about your deficiencies, until years later, you realize that you've been letting the most basic things keep you from living your best life...

Yeah, that's wack.

I'm more like the best friend you *need* to have. She's going to sound a lot like a no-nonsense Nigerian aunty who doesn't have any time to waste and loves you too much to see you waste any of your own. We've got work to do, and you have purpose to fulfill. Yesterday is dead and gone like a Justin Timberlake song, and maximizing tomorrow depends on how well you execute today.

So consider this your official warning: **This ain't a self-**_ _ **book.** Yes, I may be in the entertainment business, but I'm *not* her ·)r your entertainment. Be honest. Y'all buy those self-help books, pumped and ready to jump-start "a brand-new you," and then what happens? Five years later, those same books are doubling as coasters on your living room table. You never even made it past the first sentence of the first chapter.

I ain't going out like that.

Y'all gon'read this book. And not just read it, but apply it and activate the best you that's been lying dormant, waiting for a chance to bust out.

So *no.* This is definitely not a self-help book. **It's a GET YOURS book!**

I've gotten mine, and I'm still getting more of it. So it would be selfish of me to not share whatever I've learned along the way to help you get yours too. The prophet Nate Dogg so poignantly stated that "it ain't no fun if the homies can't get none." While he may have been referencing illicit sexual activity, that doesn't discount the wisdom of his words within the context of what *I'm* trying to say. Hopefully, by exposing you to key moments in my life, you can see for yourself that God isn't out to "get you," but He is out to get some things to you.

I'll probably hit a nerve or five and read your mail like I'm a member of Anonymous. If that happens, please don't throw the book across the room. You, or somebody who loves you very much, paid good money for it, so no need destroying perfectly good binding. Truth be told, you'll only be annoyed by what I say because it co-signs what you've been feeling or trying to suppress.

Don't fight it.

Something in your spirit is recognizing a need for change. Lean into it.

If you're wondering why I chose to parallel my life story with other stories from DGB, the short answer is, "'Cuz I thought it would be cool." Digging deeper, the Bible is a book of principles that are applicable to every aspect of life, not just the "religious" stuff. I've gained self-esteem, learned success strategies, and even understood how to stack coins from it. The principles work for anybody who works them, and you've probably already worked a few of them yourself. Take, for example, the Golden Rule, "Do unto others as you would have them do unto you." That's not just some profound, theological statement. It's a principle on how *not* to be a jerk.

This is definitely not a self-help book. It's a GET YOURS book!

Using a biblical backdrop to navigate

my journey also presented a really dope opportunity to take a book that many believe is outdated and remix its relevance. I think it's funny when people say, "I'll find faith when I'm eighty years old, after I've done all my dirt, and lived a fun life." But who said you couldn't have fun and have faith at the same darn time? I certainly do, 'cuz I don't like to choose. I'm greedy like that.

Fun and faith shouldn't be oxymorons, and the fact that they are got me thinking that perhaps, I have a different relationship with Jesus. For me, He's my homie, my road-dawg, my paht'na. Sure, He gets on my last Black nerves sometimes, but so do my other best friends. Of course, I take Him seriously, but at the same time, we still know how to kick it. He gives me room to act a fool, and when I get quiet enough to hear from Him, He lovingly (and sometimes, shadingly) corrects me.

That's the Jesus I know. But I'm not so naïve as to pretend that I don't understand how some people have a contentious relationship with the church and religion in general. They have good reason to. Humans unfortunately oversee spiritual organizations, and humans are notorious for tricking things off in the worst way. So to everyone who's ever been hurt by someone in power at a religious establishment, or made to feel unwelcome at a place of worship, I apologize on their behalf, because that's trash. If it makes you feel any better, church people killed Jesus because He wasn't churchy enough for their liking.

So again, don't feel like your lack of spiritual wisdom will hinder you from benefitting from this book. Now, if your daddy was a deacon and you sing on the praise team, don't go thinking there's nothing new you can learn from these pages. Faith builds upon faith, like the two all-beef patties on a Big Mac. Even the most familiar stories can be seen from a fresh perspective. All that's really required of you to maximize your experience with this book is to be someone who enjoys learning, laughing, and leveling up. Dassit.

But I'm getting ahead of myself. I didn't even tell you who I was or why I'm qualified to write this book, so please allow me to reintroduce myself. You already know that I'm a proud, Jesus-loving, Nigerian-American writer and stand-up comic. But in addition to that, I'm also an actress, best known as Issa Rae's BFF, Molly, on the HBO series *Insecure*. However, don't let those HBO checks fool you. They didn't come without a little stress, strain, and struggle first. I've had crosses to bear, and those heauxz were heavy. Carrie Underwood had a popular song called "Jesus Take the Wheel," and on my darkest days, I wanted Him to take the entire car: wheel, tire, exhaust pipes—all of it, 'cuz I was tih'd!

Fun and faith shouldn't be oxymorons.

If you've ever had those thoughts, then you've found your tribe. The same advice I offer, I personally had to lean on—and still reach back to apply. Many of you reading this are in some sort of transition. Maybe you're a new college grad, grappling with the daunting thought of, *What comes next?* Or you're an entrepreneur, and like me, you've found yourself in the middle of an unexpected career change, trying to navigate a whole new terrain. Perhaps you're a creative, trying to make sense of the life you chose (or were bamboozled into), while holding on to the hope that you *will* find success. No matter who you are, this:

I'm proud of you.

You probably don't hear that enough. Instead, what you get are too many people tryna place their expectations on you. They can't possibly understand the burden you bear to constantly stay grindin', stay hopeful, stay generous, *and* simultaneously stay five seconds away from *not* cussing somebody out. But I want you to know, I. SEE. YOU, because I've been you. Yes, YOU with a dream so outrageous, the possibility of it scares the crap outta you, but the thought of letting it go makes you sick to your stomach. I've also been YOU, on the verge of calling it quits, after giving it all you had. I've especially been YOU, sitting in the throngs of success, learning how to navigate a new way of life, without the familiar weight (and sometimes, safety net) of the struggle.

I'm proud of you. You probably don't hear that enough.

Nobody teaches you this stuff, or maybe they do and I just missed that class. At any rate, I believe in transparency, and that's all this book is: me exposing my trials and victories in hopes that they bring encouragement and hope to your situation. I'm fortunate to be at a point in my career where I'm sitting in the driver's seat of success, but not too far removed that my humble beginnings aren't staring back at me in the rearview mirror.

That's why I wanted to tell this story now. It's not an autobiography, by any means. At thirty-seven, I still have a lot more living to do and a lot more life to learn from. But I do feel like I've come to the natural end of phase one in my journey, and what a phase it was. There was the choosing the road less traveled section, the underdog story, the bout with depression, the pivotal moment to rally one last time, and finally arriving at the Cinderella-esque happy ending. I spare no details.

I've broken the book down into five parts: "The Burden," "The

Building," "The Breakthrough," "The Booked, Blessed, and Busy," and "The Bonus." Every part is meant to build upon the next, but you can digest the book one of two ways. If you're the type that thrives on those one-year Bible-reading plans, going from Genesis to Revelation, highlighting all over and taking notes in the margin, then have at it! You'll probably ingest this book cover to cover, and God bless you for it.

That ain't my testimony.

I'm more the type to grab the Bible, flip through pages, and stop randomly at Proverbs, to get the inspiration I need to carry me through my day. In the same way, feel free to use this as a faith fuel stop to get digestible morsels of gems being dropped in every stand-alone chapter. Depending on where you are on your journey, some chapters will resonate immediately, others will be more aspirational and you might have to tuck'em away for a later date, and there are some that you just won't vibe with at all. That's cool; my feelings aren't hurt. All I can do is share what's worked for me to get the results, but like a volunteer T-shirt, you gotta cut and style that suckka up to make it your own.

God has custom-designed your life to be magnificent, and by default, the magnificent is uncertain, daring, and downright scary. It calls you higher, forces you beyond your capacity, and demands a reckless abandon of all things safe.

There's nothing safe about this book.

Not even the title.

It's risky, and so is a magnificent life, but the only way you get one of those is

> God has custom-designed your life to be magnificent, and by default, the magnificent is uncertain, daring, and downright scary.

by allowing yourself to be bamboozled. Even though it feels like you're being punk'd, just like in the show, there was no better feeling of relief than the moment Ashton Kutcher emerged from the van, camera in hand, revealing it was all a ruse. Well, God has a reveal in store for you too. With Ashton, the payoff to his trickery was sometimes frustration, anger, or shared laughs. However, when you're bamboozled by Jesus, you'll have the last laugh. He'll have you dreaming improbable dreams, and living a life so unimaginable, you wouldn't believe it either if it wasn't your very own.

So cheers to you for believing more was possible, for trying to be the first in your family to do what was never expected, for being scared to try, but too scared *not* to. This book is for you who might be wavering in your faith as much as it is for you who are solidified in yours. Let's go get bamboozled together. The life of our dreams awaits!

THE DO'S AND DON'TS OF GETTING BAMBOOZLED

If you're like me, you love a good game night, but depending on the game (Taboo) and who you're playing with (cheating friends), you gotta set ground rules from jump. Getting bamboozled is no different. Your experience is best maximized when you know how to pick up what God is putting down, so I've outlined a few points to keep you on track.

RULE 1:
DON'T CHECK THE FINE PRINT

Are you the kind of person that actually reads all two thousand pages of Apple's terms and conditions? If so, have you considered therapy? While that may be a sign that you're fiscally responsible and a smart consumer (albeit slightly OCD), that much attention to detail ain't gon'help you get tricked into the life of your dreams.

There's definitely a fine print to getting bamboozled by Jesus, and most times we don't read it until we're in too deep. God designed it that way on purpose. If some of us read the fine print before we got started, we'd most likely renegotiate the contract or abandon ship altogether. That's why, in this case, it's best if you don't check for it at all. I surely didn't, and that's how I got *got*.

I was on the way to the club when I first met Jesus. True story. It was my freshman year of college at George Washington University, and the air was ripe for all the debauchery I intended on partaking in. As I prepared my outfit, which met the "fresh bait" curriculum—tight, leather, and short—my partner in crime, Burgette, asked if I wanted to attend a Bible study before we hit the streets, and I thought that was ironic. She was basically, *Hey, gurl, you wanna to go drop it low...but for Jesus?* I wanted to decline, but then I thought it might actually be a good look to ask for forgiveness before we got into the things we would need repentance for later. So I went.

I intended for Jesus to be a part of my college experience, just not in that moment. I had already committed to waiting until I was eighteen to have sex—which at that time was three months away. That decision, though, wasn't necessarily based on religion. It was rooted in fear. Let's just say those D.A.R.E. to keep kids off drugs and abstinence programs worked quite effectively on me. Besides, a pregnant, teenage Yvonne was not the reason my momma came to America. (She had lots of reasons why she "did not come to this country.") I figured at eighteen, I could make adult decisions, should a pregnancy arise from all the great sex I planned on having. There was even a handsome, eager, older boyfriend on deck to see the plan through. (Praise Him!)

At that point in my life, you could say that Jesus and I were cool-ish. Which would explain why I found myself at a Bible study wearing club attire. Ministering that night was a young, radical preacher named Dr. Lindsay Marsh. Lindsay and her good friend, Tameshiah, started Word Up! Bible Study as undergrads at GWU. They returned often to share how God could be a central part of our college experience, even as party-crazed, mostly broke, stressed-out students.

Lindsay intrigued me because she represented everything I wanted to be and more. She was in med school, and at the time, I thought that was part of my destiny. She was gorgeous and I longed to be pretty. Years of bullying had shattered my self-esteem. I remember once put-ting baby powder on my face in middle school both as a substitute for makeup and also as an attempt to make my dark skin lighter, since the most popular girl in my class was a caramel-butterscotch blend. My stab at becoming a beauty influencer was dead on arrival. The only thing I managed to accomplish with that Johnson & Johnson was to look a hot, ashy, ridiculous mess—and getting bullied some more.

Beyond her beauty, Lindsay loved God with such an unshakable passion that it made me want that same level of intimacy with Him too. She was twenty-six and a virgin and I also wanted to be twenty...wait, what?!

Time out. Flag on the play.

Why would anybody wanna do that? I certainly wasn't about that life, not with three months left on my countdown. But as I sat in Word Up!, tryna make my skirt feel longer, something started tugging at my heart. Was the love of God she spoke of the acceptance I'd been search-ing for this whole time? I thought it would come from the cliques I sought to be a part of, but could it come from a Savior who was willing to accept me as-is, like clearance items at Ross? And all I had to do was say a prayer? What was the catch?

As someone who grew up Catholic, I thought I knew God. I was used to fourty-five-minute sermons—an hour tops, if the priest was feeling himself, or if announcements went long. I was baptized Catholic, received my first holy communion, recited the rosary daily, and went to confession frequently. But it turned out that what I really knew was tradition and formula. No shade to Catholicism, but I didn't know JESUS.

Not the way Lindsay knew Him: Personally. Intimately. Lovingly. It was almost like they were friends, but who's *friends* with Jesus? She even went as far as calling God "Daddy." At that point I thought, *Yo, this chick got daddy issues.* But I was curious. Lindsay went on to say that it was God's love for her that made it a simple choice to surrender her life to His will. I didn't know what all that meant, but I knew that I at least wanted to try to give Him my all. It seemed to be working out alright for her. From that moment on, I gave God my uninhibited "yes," and nothing was ever the same, like a Drake album.

So much for my big plans at eighteen. Talk about a setup! Sure, at seventeen, it *sounded* good to commit to remaining a virgin until I was married, but what happens when the fine print still has me single at thirty-seven? You download every dating app, that's what! No, seriously, in my case, I have to keep trusting that there is a man out there who's tailor-made just for me, no matter how long it takes (but, like for real tho, hurry up).

In Da Good Book, Joseph "the dreamer" didn't even know there was fine print to be read until he was living in it, and by then, there was no turning back. God had already gotten him hooked on the promise, so the only thing left to do was to ride out the pain to get to purpose. If you've ever watched the DreamWorks movie *The Prince of Egypt*, then you sorta already know Joe's story. Essentially, he was one of the youngest brothers in a large family. Errybody knew he was his daddy's favorite, and that caused some of haideration with his older siblings. It didn't help that, out of all his sons, Jacob gave Joseph a fly, couture, Dapper Dan Gucci jacket to rock around the crib. To make matters worse, God told Joe in a dream that his brothers—who already didn't like him— would eventually bow down to him. Joe then had the audacity to share the dream with his bros—who already didn't like him. Bruh, what is you doing?!

Even though he didn't fully understand the dream, JoJo was naïve enough to believe it. But no one told him that the dream God sold him on would eventually get him sold into slavery by his own brothers, falsely accused of sexual harassment by his boss's wife, and thrown into prison and forgotten for years, before finally coming true when he was made vice president of Egypt.[1] That's how getting bamboozled by Jesus works. You believe the dream, get hooked on hope, then get sucker-punched by the fine print, before eventually winning the prize. I know this blueprint well, 'cuz God has used it on me several times, like when I moved to New York.

Taking that leap of faith was definitely the right thing to do, but thank God I didn't read the fine print about how my decision would cause a strain in my family for almost eight years, or the immense poverty I would experience while I watched my friends buy houses, get married, and have kids. Fortunately, I didn't let any of those factors

---

1. See Genesis 37.

deter me, because if I had, I'd be missing out on the life I'm currently living, and you'd be missing out on all the nuggets in this book.

We can't ask Joseph if he was resentful of his brothers. We'll never know if he was livid at Potiphar's wife. We'll always wonder if he was bitter after being forgotten in the jail cell.

No, we can't ask him how he felt in those moments, but you can ask me. I'll tell you that it sucked feeling let down, betrayed, and on the verge of hopelessness. I'm guessing it's not unlike how you might be feeling in your own situation: I don't know your particular adjectives, but I have a few others for you: vindicated, restored, purposeful, happy. This is what it feels like to get to the other side of your mountain.

If Joseph knew everything he would go through just by having that dream, he might've asked for nightmares instead, but if you think about it, every last one of Joe's perceived setbacks actually served a purpose to getting him *to* purpose. Let's run it back. If Joe never got sold to Potiphar, then he wouldn't have had experience working under an important ruler. And if he never got that experience, then he might've choked under the pressure of working for King Pharaoh and gotten fired. And if he'd gotten fired, then he wouldn't have been in his position when his brothers came to Egypt to buy food. And if he wasn't in his position, then they never would've bowed down to him like he saw in his dream all those years earlier. In a way, you could look at the series of unfortunate events in Joseph's life as an unpaid internship preparing him for his destiny.

> You could look at the series of unfortunate events in Joseph's life as an unpaid internship preparing him for his destiny.

So do yourself a favor—don't go looking for the fine print. It'll find you eventually. And when it does, stay the course. Yes, it may seem like the world is conspiring against you, but it's not. Those are just hidden details that were built into the contract of your life. They're all necessary to get you to exactly where you're meant to be.

RULE 2:
DO ALLOW GOD TO ADD
HIS SUPER TO YOUR NATURAL

Of all the superheroes, I roxx with Superman the most. In the natural, Superman's alter-ego, Clark Kent, seems like your average, run-of-the-mill kinda guy. He has a nine-to-five, lives in a rent-controlled apartment, and wears Old Navy khakis—fairly ordinary stuff. But when danger strikes and it's time for Superman to come on the scene, he adds his extra to Clark Kent's ordinary to become the extraordinary force that saves the day. That's what God does with us. He takes our natural abilities, ideas, and gifts and adds His super to them. I say all the time that I'm not the smartest, most talented, prettiest, or funniest entertainer out there, and you know what? That's okay. Don't get me wrong, I'm pretty great, but I have my limitations, just like you do. But when I show up, flaws and all, God powers up in my life and makes all of me enough for every single moment.

I heard Pastor Steven Furtick say, "If I use what I've got, then God'll help me be what I'm not!" The question is: "What've you got?" Do you know? Do you protect it? Do you harness it to produce more, or do you discount it because it seems insignificant? If Jesus disregarded the things we deem basic about ourselves, He wouldn't have had any disciples. To the natural eye, they were all a band of misfits. Take Peter for instance. He was your average fisherman. Not exactly the most remark-able or obvious choice to kick it with the Son of Man, but Peter actually had a few qualities that made him a legit candidate to be Jesus' right-hand man.

For starters, he was diligent at his job. When Jesus ordered him to throw his nets into the sea to catch some fish, Peter told Jesus straight up that he'd worked all night and still hadn't caught anything.[2] Maybe it was that drive that Jesus saw in Peter to make him think, *Yup, I can work with this.* Peter also showed humility and flexibility in his ability to adapt to new ideas. Even though he was burnt out from an unsuc-cessful catch, he still decided to give Jesus a shot and said, "Because You say so, I will let down my nets." Imagine what God can do in your life with a "because you say so" kinda attitude. That'll be the game changer in your bamboozled journey. Let's recap Peter's résumé in a rather short interaction with Jesus: He (1) was a persistent worker, (2) was able to take direction, and (3) respected leadership. Sure, he was a little reckless at times, but chalk that up to him being passionate.

Where many of us would've seen a smelly fisherman, Jesus saw someone He could mold to make a fisher of men. So please don't dis-credit what God can use to your credit. Even through this book process, I've had to take my own advice. I messed around and made the mistake of listening to Bishop T. D. Jakes speak while I was writing. He uses words that make me question the validity of my entire vocabulary and make me feel so inadequate. But I decided that my job isn't to pull out every SAT word I ever learned. It's to write coherent sentences that con-nect with my reader and tell a compelling story. The rest is up to Jesus. His name is on the cover, so it's in His best interest to make it good.

2. See Luke 5:5.

In 2 Thessalonians, it says that "God gives you everything you need…[and he'll] make you fit for what he's called you to be…he'll fill your good ideas and acts of faith with his own energy so that it all amounts to something" (1:2, 11–12 MSG). That right there makes me want to shout, "Keep that same energy, Jesus!" And the reality is, He will. So go ahead and do your part in the natural, and watch God supersize it.

Don't discredit what God can use to your credit.

RULE 3:
DO LET GOD BUILD AN ACCESSIBLE RAMP

I was watching an episode of the Hulu show *Ramy*, where Ramy and his friends arrive at a house and quickly realize that their buddy who uses a wheelchair won't be able to scale the stairs leading up to the house. That's when the band of brothers huddles together to lift their friend inside. We've all been that friend who's needed a boost. Each one of us has some sort of barrier or circumstance that impedes our progress. At times, these disabilities present as emotional, physical, or financial deficits. While we might see them as a disadvantage, God sees them as opportunities. He takes our special needs and becomes the ramp to get us over every hurdle.

In DGB, the folks God used to accomplish great things suffered from one shortcoming or another. They deemed themselves as less than perfect and, thus, disqualified for what God had in store. What they failed to realize is that God doesn't choose the perfect; He perfects the chosen. Look at Moses. He went down in history as a great leader who freed the Israelites from captivity. However, his disability was that he had a stuttering problem. Apparently, Hooked on Phonics didn't work for him.

You can imagine his reluctance when God instructed him to use *all* of his words to command an entire nation. Moses responded with a smooth "Nah, I'm good." He was so paralyzed by fear that he straight up asked God to pick somebody else to fulfill His purpose. Before you start clowning, Mo, think back on how many times you've begged God to forfeit His plans for your life 'cuz you've got a couple of shortcomings. No one's judging you. We've all done it. The truth is, God needs our broke down, no good, shameful, and imperfect. If we had it all together, there'd be no need for Him to work miracles in us.

Abraham and Sarah, in Da Good Book, saw firsthand how God could turn their broke down into a breakthrough. They were promised a daycare full of kids, but at ninety years old, Sarah was hecka infertile, and there was no in vitro—wasn't a thing. One day, God told Sarah she was gon' be pregnant with a son by the following year.[3] Thinking He was joking, Sarah just laughed in His face, like, "Boy, please!" I love how God responded to her insufficiency with His Supremacy when He asked, "Is there anything too hard for the Lord?"[4]

In my case, I *did* think it would be too hard for God to make me confident in my funny. The trauma from being bullied as a kid still screams at me loudly, and tries to convince me that someway, somehow, I'll be rejected onstage for all to see; never mind the fact that I've successfully been doing stand-up since 2006. I scoffed like Sarah when God told me the impact my humor would have. Like Moses, I looked

---

3. See Genesis 18:10.
4. See Genesis 18:14.

for a way out, pleading with God to use something less terrifying to get me to my purpose.

While I was busy trying to rid myself of the discomfort of my insecurities, God was busy using them to open doors and usher me into new rooms. I still get nervous from time to time, but the difference is, I've learned to lean into my shortcomings and own the heck outta them. They're what makes me enjoy other people's gifts and seek out community. Oh, and in case you're wondering, Sarah did get pregnant the following year and she and Abraham had a bushel of decendants. God had the last laugh after all.

> *God needs our broke down, no good, shameful, and imperfect.*

RULE 4:
DO SHOW UP SO GOD CAN SHOW OFF

As a little kid, I loved watching the animated series *G.I. Joe*. Every episode ended with a public service announcement where a group of kids learned an important life lesson and responded with, "Now we know," and a *G.I. Joe* officer would reply, "And knowing is half the battle." Now that I'm full grown, life has taught me that *showing up* is actually half the battle. The other half is showing up prepared.

There's a story in DGB about ten virgins who showed up to meet an eligible bachelor. Five of them came prepared with extra oil for their lamps, and the other five were foolish goats who arrived with just enough for the journey. Sure enough, #BachelorBae was late, and the five chicks that started with the bare minimum were almost tapped out. They begged the prepared five to pour out a lil' oil for the homies, but those ladies hit'em with a Destiny's Child, "No, No, No, No, NO!" and suggested they hurry to the corner store before Bae arrived. While they were gone, homeboy showed up, looking fine as wine, and took the five available girls to a VIP lounge. When the other girls arrived at the spot, madd late, security promptly escorted them off the premises.[5]

How many of us have been tardy to our own party? We're showing up late or not showing up at all to receive blessings that were preordained for us. Well, that ends today. While other people are checking out, or running to regroup, we gon'be the ones to inherit the promise if for no other reason than the fact that WE SHOWED UP! #BachelorBae only took the girls he found waiting. Nothing was said about them being prettier than the other girls. We have no idea if they were better cooks or super outgoing. They were just *there* when it was time to be there, and prepared when it was time to go. In our own lives, we have to do our part and show up, so God can do His part and show off.

When I decided to move to New York to work in entertainment, I didn't have much planned out. I'd saved $500 to take an acting class that cost $450, and used the extra money for a bus ticket, but I still didn't have a place to stay yet. On the bus, I called everyone I knew in the city and posted on Facebook that I was looking for a couch to crash on. Halfway to Manhattan, I got a message from Jacque Khoury telling me to call her immediately. I barely knew Jacque. We'd met only once when I worked in Liberia, so what did she want to talk to me so urgently about?

Turns out Jacque had seen my post and wanted to offer me the basement apartment in her home. I ended up living with her and her

---

5. See Matthew 25:1–13.

family rent-free for six months. That's unheard of. When I think back on it, that blessing was already lined up, but there would've been no reason for God to pull the trigger on it if I was still chilling in Maryland, afraid to make a bold move of faith. Start now to show God you mean business, and He'll show you His many blessings.

We have to do our part and show up, so God can do His part and show off.

Practice this in big and small ways. Show up to the event when they say it's sold out. You never know who's got an extra ticket with your name on it. Show up to the staff meeting knowing as much as your supervisor. That just might be the day your boss asks you to present. Show up to do community service work. Your future spouse might be right there, ready to give back.

RULE 5:
DON'T NEGLECT THE "SMALL" STUFF

While many of us trust that God'll show up in the big moments, we shouldn't discount His care for the trivial desires of our hearts. If it matters to you, it matters to Him. Here's proof. Da Good Book says that God knows the number of hairs on your head. Well, why else would He go through the trouble of counting every follicle if He didn't want to be intimately connected with you? If your biological father only showed up at major moments of your life, I suppose y'all could still have a decent relationship—but there would be so much missed. True intimacy comes from the little moments, like piggyback rides and practicing jump shots. God not only wants to be invited to these tender times, He actually looks forward to them.

My first Christmas in LA, I decided to get a live Christmas tree. Growing up, my parents were not about that pine-needles-on-their-carpet life, so artificial trees were all I knew. I had a vision to have my crisp, green tree up against a chocolate brown wall. Problem was, I was living off a production assistant's salary, and paint ain't cheap. In the hierarchy of essential bills that needed my financial attention, paint was more of a luxury than a necessity. The weekend I was set to pick out my tree was fast approaching, but every time I looked at the white wall of my apartment, I grew more frustrated.

A few days later at work, I was asked to make a run to Lowe's to grab some office supplies. While in the store, I remembered how my former pastor, Mike Freeman, would encourage us to get God's attention by doing things that activated our faith. So rather than telling myself I couldn't afford paint, I strolled down the paint aisle just to *see* if they had the chocolate shade of paint I wanted. And y'aaaal, not only did they have the *exact* shade, but God did me one better. The cans were discounted from $40 to $4! Come thru Jesus!

He's the author of time and doesn't need it micromanaged by anyone.

There are some things you might think are insignificant to bring to God, like paint on sale. You convince yourself that He has bigger prayers to answer and you don't want to bother Him or waste His time. While I'm sure God appreciates your concern, please understand that He's the author of time and doesn't need it micromanaged by anyone.

Before you can get bamboozled by Jesus, you first have to grant God access into the intricate spaces of your life. Maybe that looks like asking Him which college to attend, or having Him help you shake the nerves off before a first date. Whatever it is, He's not too busy and you're not a nuisance. He actually likes to sweat the small stuff.

● ● ●

Now that you're hip to game, you're ready to tackle the next phase of getting bamboozled. It'll require a lil' blind trust and surrender. I personally don't trust trust falls. But the good news is that God's a pretty good catch. Take your time, pace yourself, and stretch your mind. There's no finish line to cross, and you're not in competition with anyone but yourself.

PART I

The Burden

CHAPTER 1

I Am What I Am

Who I am is a concept I've struggled with for a long time. When I was young, I became so many things to so many people, all for the sake of fitting in. In school, I became the smart kid, 'cuz you can't be both foolish and friendless. Wheretheydodatat? I relished being smart, 'cuz for those brief moments in science class, when I let the pretty girls copy my homework, I believed I was one of them. No matter how fleeting the moment was, I felt needed. Necessary. Important.

At home, I was expected to be "the good Nigerian girl." That basically meant: Make straight A's, go to church, learn to cook, wash dishes ('cuz our dishwasher was basically a drying rack), don't date, graduate from college, head to med school, and somehow, suddenly discover the existence of boys, get married, and have two to four kids, all by the tender age of twenty-eight. This, to my parents and Nigerian culture at large, was my reasonable service for the sacrifices they'd made in bringing me and my three older brothers to America. At the age of six this was the burden that was placed on me—disguised as duty and destiny.

I was following the good Nigerian girl protocol to the T, especially when it came to education. That was my parents' top priority. I used to think we were poor the way they shut down requests for frivolous things that required money, like recreation and fun, but somehow all of us Orji kids managed to attend private boarding high schools. I remember once getting a B on my report card and hiding out in the woods by our house, too afraid to go home and reveal the shame I'd brought on our family name. There's no denying the fact I was a "people pleaser," and by people, I mean my parents. Back then, most of my decision-making came down to this simple criteria:

A. Would it make Mom and Dad mad?
B. Would Mom and Dad be proud of it/me?
C. How bad of a whooping would this get me?

Option B was the only thing I lived for.

Becoming a doctor would've been the ultimate personification of the American Dream for my folks. A lot of people ask why African parents, especially Nigerians, harp on their kids being doctors, lawyers, or engineers. The short answer is: Bragging rights. Nothing brings Nigerian parents more joy than having a conversation like this:

In Accent
Mom: My dear, how are you?
Friend: You know, my arthritis is acting up, but other than that, I'm fine. How are the children?
Mom: Oh, they are all well. In fact, join me in thanking God

for His goodness and mercy. Justina got admission into
HAAVAAD (Harvard) Medical School.

Friend: You don't mean it?! Wow, God has really blessed you with
a child who will care for you in your old age.

Mom: Amen o! I'm so grateful. It's very unfortunate how your
own children turned out. But don't worry, I'll be praying
for you.

Because bragging always tastes better with a tall glass of shade.

Seriously, though, beyond bragging, I actually think the answer
lies in the fact that there's no Social Security, Medicaid, or Obamacare
back home, where the health care facilities are subpar at best. Therefore,
many parents aspire to have at least one doctor in the family to care for
them. Also, being a doctor is a symbol of hard work and intelligence—
basically, the bedrock of being a Nigerian. You're welcome, Ghana.

The summer before I started high school, my family took our
annual trip to Nigeria. What started as a routine catch-up with cousins, culture, and cuisine, ended with tragedy. One of my aunts had an
ectopic pregnancy, which is when the fetus grows in the fallopian tube
rather than the uterus. As you can imagine, serious health risks are associated with that. Even though she was rushed to the hospital, the doctor
refused to perform lifesaving surgery because he couldn't guarantee my
aunt could afford it. Hours later, when we arrived, my mother quickly
jumped into nurse mode, and my dad berated the surgeon.

My aunt survived but lost the baby. Looking at her sobbing in her
hospital room, my twelve-year-old self made a vow, right then and there,
that I would be the one to give my parents the doctor they longed for.

Circumstances like these would never happen again. Not on my watch! I was determined, and nothing was going to stop me...

Except maybe organic chemistry.

Y'all, I tried! I really did, but organic chemistry is an enemy of progress. When I saw that F on my transcript—and it wasn't for "fantastic"—I was shook. It meant that I wouldn't be getting into the Early Acceptance Program, a fast-track plan to med school offered at GWU. It also let me know with the quickness that I needed to find another way to take care of my parents. Looking back now, I realize, like my birth story, that was another one of God's interceptions. His not-so-subtle nudge guiding me toward *His* plans for my life. However, at the time, I hadn't yet mastered the delicate art of prioritizing God over pleasing my parents.

Maybe I'd known medicine wasn't for me all along. Nothing about being a doctor was remotely appealing to me, other than actually being called a doctor; and even *that* was problematic. I mean, my last name is Orji. Imagine hearing, "Paging Dr. Orji. Dr. Orji!" Listen, I'd already been picked on as a kid. I wasn't about to voluntarily carry that into adulthood. On top of my super-suspect surname, I also hate the sight of blood. It's pretty remarkable how I make it through a menstrual cycle each month. Seriously, every twenty-eight days, I'm like, *This again? How many eggs am I dropping? Sheesh!*

I should have known medicine wasn't my jam from the start, because as a kid, I used books as my escape from the loneliness of friendlessness. I'd borrow twelve books at a time from the public library, which my mom promptly warned me to finish (because paying late fees was also not the reason she came to America). I devoured *Goosebumps* and got lost in the world of *Sweet Valley High*. Maybe that's why I decided to major in sociology rather than biology in college. It was easier to write fifty-page term papers than struggle to understand covalent bonds. We all have those mustard-seed moments of our true purpose seeping through. They betray our well-laid plans, and we often dismiss them because they're extremely subtle, but they never truly go away. They're just lying dormant, waiting to be discovered and cultivated.

I loved all the possibilities created from reading, but no one ever told me that being a writer or an actor was an actual profession. Sure, I knew that words had to get on the page somehow, but it didn't dawn on me that somebody got paid cold, hard cash to put them there. There's a lot that I didn't know then—like maybe I was falling in love with stories because one day I would be called to write my own. God is strategic like that.

After the abysmal F, uncertain of which path to take, I found it easier to keep dodging the truth rather than let my parents down. Also, I had no backup plan. How would that conversation even go? *"Hey, Mom and Dad, I know for the last twenty-one years, you thought I was going to be this one thing, but, yeah, that's not gon'work for me anymore. No idea what I'll do instead, but I just know it ain't gon'be that. Good chat!"* Have you met Nigerian parents? They would've had my tail on a one-way ticket back to Lagos with the quickness. So I thugged it out and did the only logical thing to do:

Stall.

And I kept stalling. After undergrad, I got my master's in public health, because the only thing Nigerians love more than education is more education. You've heard of *The Five Love Languages*? Well, for Nigerians, there's a sixth: degrees. It's the way to our heart. Right around this time, I stumbled into stand-up. And by stumbled, I mean Jesus bamboozled me into performing comedy under the guise of "trusting" Him. I told you about those trust falls. Unsure of how anyone survived on a comic's salary, I allowed my parents to believe that my newfound passion was nothing more than a hobby. But, I couldn't shake the feeling of finally finding my voice and the thrill of being responsible for the laughter of strangers. Three years went by, and with degree number two in hand, the question resurfaced: "*Now* are you going to med school?"

Nope. Still gon' stall.

This time, stalling took me halfway across the globe to Liberia, working for a nonprofit organization. Liberia had just finished a brutal civil war and the country was a hotbed for development efforts. In case you're not tracking, lemme break it down for you. I was such a punk, and so deathly afraid of disappointing my parents, that I'd rather move to a war-torn country than to actually confess that I no longer wanted to be the one thing they desperately wanted me to be. It was ridiculous, I know. But that's exactly what I did. And it's no different to what you might be doing right now—maybe not as drastic, but equally as effective in delaying the inevitable.

For six months, I lived in Liberia and enjoyed the safety net of avoidance until my contract expired (or I got fired—depends on who's telling the story; My book, soooo…contract expired). I returned to Maryland at the height of the 2009 recession and discovered that nobody else had a job. While everyone else seemed devastated by it, the recession was literally the best thing to ever happen to me. I know that sounds insane but think about it: Since no one would think it strange that a dual-degree-having Nigerian-American girl would trade a life in corporate America to become a soon-to-be starving artist, it was the perfect decoy.

Armed with that kind of ammunition, I bet on Black and bought a one-way bus ticket to New York City. Of course, that meant that I finally had to confess to my parents that their dream would indefinitely be deferred like a Langston Hughes poem. I explained that I'd prayed about it and truly believed this was the path God wanted me to follow. To which my dad angrily retorted, "God? You think you're the only one that prays to God? Before you were born, were we not also praying to Him?" (Deng, I couldn't even play the God card!) With nothing left in the chamber, I said that I just had to try. If I failed, then at least I would go out knowing I gave it my all. I suggested an ultimatum where they'd allow me eight years to make it as a stand-up, which is roughly the length of time it takes to finish med school and residency. If things didn't work out, then I agreed to come back home, find any job, and marry a Nigerian doctor. Thankfully, I made it in seven years! Look at God looking out!

Before I left, tears were shed by all. My parents cried because they felt betrayed by me, and I wept because I felt the strange mix of being so misunderstood, and yet for the first time, feeling so free. That one act of defiance started me on the very long journey of giving God many uncertain yeses in exchange for achieving several improbable dreams. There's a guy in Da Good Book named Paul, who knows all about surrendering a "yes" to get God's best.

Before Jesus changed his name, Paul was called Saul, and Saul was kind of a jerk. Scratch that, he was a tyrant. He hated Christians and killed as many of them as possible. One day, he was on his way to perform his next drive-by, but Jesus intercepted his plans and blinded him. But instead of retaliating against Saul for all the havoc he'd caused, Jesus hit up his homeboy, Ananias, and asked him to take care of Saul because, as He put it, Saul was His chosen instrument, whom He intended on using to spread the Good News.[1]

Pause. How could the same man that was taking out God's people become the same guy God wanted to use as a mouthpiece for the Gospel? That's some kind of reckless love, but that's legit how I be feeling sometimes when I think about how, out of the eight billion people on Earth, God desires to use me, *a whole me,* for an unfathomable purpose. Many times I've asked God, "But, like, why me, though?" I'm the youngest in my family. I wasn't one of the cool kids, and I really don't have much to offer except for a coupl'a yeses.

Saul could certainly relate because when he converted to become the Apostle Paul, he declared "I am the least of the apostles and"—real talk—"do not even deserve to be called an apostle...." But here's the part that gets me every time. After he owned his shortcomings, he still had the confidence of mind to boldly proclaim, "But by the grace of God I am what I am."[2] Paul didn't waste precious time and energy self-analyzing, self-sabotaging, or self-loathing, like I sometimes do. He called it like he saw it. "I *know* I've done some foul stuff. I know I've been trash. But that was the old me, and all that matters is that, by the grace of God, I am what I am."

Despite his disposition, I imagine it still wasn't easy for Paul to convert the same folks he used to kill. That's why God had to change his name. He needed Paul to not have to answer to the old him, because, like an app, that version had been updated and all the bugs fixed. Still, I'm sure people talked crap about him because they remembered what he did as Saul. I'm positive they used his past as receipts to deem him unworthy of the call God placed on his life.

---

1. See Acts 9:1–16.
2. 1 Corinthians 15:9–10 NIV.

You prolly know some of these people. You got a coupl'a them in your family, at work, or at school. Their sole purpose is to remind you of who you were, where you aren't, and what you ain't gon'do. They tell you, "You're too old to try that. Too fat to be that. Too Black to own that, too short, too nice, too poor, too smart." You name it and you're probably too *it* to be that. Shoot, if they kept going, you'd be too YOU to be you. And you know what? They might be right! But when has any of that ever stopped God's plans?

I was twenty-five years old when I started from the bottom in entertainment. Various members of my family tried to convince me that I'd missed my window of opportunity. They loved reminding me that most people usually started when they were teenagers. And they weren't wrong. I knew I was older, but I also knew I had a promise from Jesus, and by the grace of God, I am what I am, and I make it do what it does.

Make no mistake, anytime you own the fullness of who you are, it'll make others uncomfortable. They'll talk bad about you and try to poke holes in your transformation. Let 'em talk. Opinions are like booty holes; errybody got one. They're entitled to have them, just like you're entitled not to let 'em faze you.

I wondered why Jesus called Paul an "instrument," though. Wasn't there a more powerful word He could've used, like "soldier" or "warrior"? That sounds more noble. But He said plain old "instrument." It made more sense after I looked it up. Turns out, an instrument is defined as "a means whereby something is achieved, performed, or furthered."

Achieved. Performed. Furthered.

> Opinions are like booty holes; errybody got one.

Sounds a lot like what Paul did in his ministry. He achieved glory for God, performed good works, and furthered the Gospel. But Paul's not the only one that gets dibs on these special privileges. Da Good Book says that you and I are meant to be "instruments for special purposes, made holy, useful to the Master and prepared to do any good work."[3] Basically, God is setting us up for peak performance. He's purging our pasts and purifying our presents in order for us to receive the fullness of our futures.

If you're vacillating between giving a "yes" that you know will advance your purpose or staying stuck in the quicksand of doubt and uncertainty, lemme encourage you to go balls to the wall and dive all-in. You can't see it now, but every "yes" you give God aligns you with the next set of hurdles and triumphs that'll catapult you one step closer to purpose. The crazy thing is, half the time, your "yes" ain't even about you.

When God gives you an audacious dream, it's often attached to the benefit of others. In my own life, my defiance has started a bit of a chain reaction. The same parents, who used to have random strangers call to convince me to give up my "pipe dreams," now have me call other Nigerian parents to convince them to allow their children to study the arts. Talk about a full-circle moment. But they wouldn't have had that opportunity had I not pressed in to obtain the promise. You may have no idea how things will work out, but I do know that someone is waiting on your "yes," so they can eat off the fruit of your obedience, and declare, "But by the grace of God, I am what I am!"

---

3. 2 Timothy: 2:21 NIV.

CHAPTER 2

PLAY YO' POSITION

I can't sing. Not even a little bit. Whenever I ask someone if they know a song, and try to sing it to them, I'm almost always met with, "Never heard of it." It's not until I play the actual song that they exclaim, "Oh, I know *that* song, but what were *you* singing?" I'm convinced that had God blessed me with a good singing voice, I'd be a stripper. My stripper name would be Chocolate Testimony, 'cuz I'd be droppin' it low while droppin' da Word! Don't ask me why that correlation; it just feels right. It's the same reason why I can't have six-pack abs. I would be reckless in these skreetz; showing up to church with nothing but pasties and crop tops, bodyrolling to the altar. Jesus knew I couldn't be trusted with nice things, so He keeps me with a humble pouch and a garbage disposal for vocal cords.

My tone-deafness never actually *stops* me from singing, much to my friends' annoyance. I don't know how or why I became this relentless, but it goes all the way back to elementary school. We would have talent shows, which were more like lip-sync battles before LL Cool J made them, well…*cool*. Groups of friends would sign up to act out hits from SWV to Bone Thugs-N-Harmony. The fact that no one ever signed up to perform with me didn't stop me from picking an R&B group with four members and singing all the different parts by. my. self. The "boooos" I received when I grabbed the mic didn't deter my resilience either. Each year, I was ever so certain that *this* would be the year I'd win the critics over.

I never did.

But I never grew tired of trying. So you would think then that when Holy Spirit prompted me to "do comedy" for the first time at the 2016 Miss Nigeria in America Pageant, I would've jumped at the chance to grab the mic one mo'gain. But that's not how things went down. I'd signed up to compete, not because I was the pageant type, but because I was free on a Saturday and was doing a favor for my brother, whose friend ran the competition.

Two weeks before the big day, I got a phone call I wasn't expecting: *Hey, Yvonne, looking over your application, you haven't listed your act for the talent portion and you can't compete without one.* Of course I didn't have a talent. As children of immigrants, we aren't raised to engage in extracurricular activities. The only thing I was good at was making the Dean's List, and you can't really perform that onstage.

Unfortunately, I'd already bought a gown, and friends and family had already purchased tickets, so I was in too deep to back out. At that point, I knew three things to be true: (1) I wasn't going to sing; (2) the last thing I'd learned to play on the piano was "Mary Had a Little Lamb," so that wasn't gonna cut it; and (3) I wasn't about to be tribal dancing on anybody's stage in front of my momma and all her friends. So I called in a lifeline. It was a simple prayer: *Dear sweet baby*

Jesus, sleeping in a manger, HEEEEEELLLPPP!! Amen. Before my knees had a chance to rise from the carpet, loud as day, I heard the still, small voice of Holy Spirit saying, *"Do comedy."*

I knew it had to be the Spirit, because it certainly wasn't *my* idea. What did that even mean, *Do comedy*? Was I funny? I'd never performed stand-up a day in my life, nor did I desire to, and I wasn't about to start now when I actually had something to lose, besides my dignity. Couldn't God see that the first thing audiences do to unfunny comics is boo? This wasn't elementary school when I was desperate to win the approval of my peers. I was in grad school now. I'd made friends. I was part of the in-crowd and I planned on keeping it that way.

To make matters worse, the auditorium would be filled with Nigerians, and we are the rudest people you will ever encounter. Booing would actually be a courtesy—a luxury even. If Nigerians are displeased, they will either start loudly talking over you, answer a call from overseas, or slowly dismantle your soul with their utter disregard of your presence, while yelling out, "Whose daughter is this?"

Naturally, being the faith-filled woman that I am, when I heard, *"Do comedy,"* I responded like a true believer and said: "Nah!"

Sure did.

I told Jesus to try again and do better. I couldn't see how His plan would work because I was more focused on the embarrassment I would face if I bombed than the future I would inherit if I succeeded. My mind kept looping a tape of people laughing at, not with, me, and my mom covering her face in shame. Any remnants of elementary-school me were fading fast. In the middle of my righteous indignation of telling Jesus what I wasn't gon'do, I heard Holy Spirit say, *"Alright then, what else you got?"* Oh c'mon, Jesus! You don't play fair. You know I ain't *got nothing!* He then responded with, *"Well, either you're gonna learn to trust Me, or you're not."*

That was it. God wasn't going back and forth with me. He was drawing a line in the sand and it was up to me to decide what kind of relationship we were gon'have. Would it be one of convenience—where I interacted based on how things benefitted me, or would it be a partnership—where I surrendered to *His* will? Was I gonna play my position as a child of God and trust that He knew more than me, or was I gonna succumb to fear, play it safe, and back out?

It was a tight spot to be in, but I knew I didn't want to play church—I didn't want to say I believed with my words, but not show it with my actions. What was the point of that? If I was going to do this Christianity thing, then I wanted access to the full benefits. Anything less would be a waste of errybody's time.

I guess talent-show Yvonne was still in there somewhere, itching to bust loose. Or maybe all those years ago, she was just preparing me for what was to come. There she was in that moment, reminding me of a time when I didn't care what anyone else thought, when I dared to be so bold and live out loud, without consequence. The younger me had done so, not because faith required it of her, but because she knew her plight would be temporary. After eighth grade, I knew I was going to boarding school, never to see the likes of anyone at Oakland Elementary or Eisenhower Middle School ever again.

The pageant would also be temporary. A blip in time. A moment where I did a thing. But maybe it frightened me more because it wasn't my idea. With the lip-syncs, I knew my strengths and chose my selections accordingly. Furthermore, those songs were already popular. Someone else had done the heavy lifting of ensuring they would be a hit. I was just mouthing words. But the pageant was different. I was being asked to play a position I wasn't sure I was qualified for, and I would be held responsible if I failed.

Agreeing to what God has for you sets you up to be used in both rewarding and terrifying ways. (How's that for motivation?) Your participation will be requested at times that aren't convenient with your schedule, in ways that don't fit your five-year plan, and in moments where you won't think you're the most qualified (wo)man for the job. The good news is, it's not about you, boo. God's not picking you to get bamboozled because you're so bomb. He wants to use you so you'll be molded into an even better version of yourself, and grow to have a deeper understanding of Him.

That's what happened to a chick named Esther in Da Good Book. Like Cardi B, Esther was just a regula, degula, shmegula girl from a middle-class family. She was busy minding her own business when, one day, God changed her entire life. King Xerxes had just sent his wife, Vashti, packing, with everything she owned in a box to the left. To cheer him up, his boys scooped up all the young virgins in town for him to pick the best one to be the next one, and that's how Esther became queen.

But here's the catch: Esther was a Jew, and the Jews and Xerxes' people didn't always get along. To protect her, her uncle Mordecai told her to keep her identity a secret. As it turned out,

> God's not picking you to get bamboozled because you're so bomb. He wants to use you so you'll be molded into an even better version of yourself.

Haman, the king's right-hand man, had beef with Mordecai, so he convinced Xerxes to issue a law to eradicate all the Jews. When Mordecai told Esther what types of games were being played in the palace and urged her to get her husband's help, she responded from a place of comfort, privilege, and fear of giving up all of that comfort and privilege. Clearly, Esther had heard through the grapevine what had happened with Vashti, and she wasn't tryna go out like the trash on a Thursday. Liiissseeen, I get it. If I were in Esther's position, I'd be a little hesitant too. Who wants to go back on the dating scene after you've been married to the king? It's hard out here for a single woman tryna find a good man! Who else on Tinder gon'have royal servants? Eggzaklee.

The problem is, a life of purpose is rarely one where you get to skate by unfazed, untested, or unchallenged. Esther made the mistake of thinking her special status as queen exempted her from participating in God's plan for her life. I mean, sure, she was pretty, but pretty is disposable. And, yeah, you're talented, but talent is manufacturable. There'll always be someone better skilled creeping on the come up. When all you are is special, you can be replaced. But when you're available, you're already standing in position, so no one can take your place.

Esther being selected for greatness was less a reflection of her amazingness and more a statement of God's strategic positioning. He only needed her willing participation and He would handle the rest. Unfortunately, Esther had gotten pacified by pleasure. If we're being honest, sometimes we, too, get complacent with comfort. I know I have. Before that pageant, I was comfortable (albeit unfulfilled) being the good Nigerian girl. I knew what was expected of me, and I wasn't prepared to ruffle any feathers. Thankfully, Esther had good ol' Uncle Mordi to snatch her back to reality, in what I call a Mordecai Moment. He told her not to think for a second that God wouldn't raise up someone else to help them. So it wasn't that the Jews *needed* her; they were simply offering her an opportunity to get in on God's master plan. Your willingness isn't doing God any favors, but it does open up doors of favor toward you.

I don't know about you, but the thought that God could call me to do something potentially magnificent, and through my inaction or willful disobedience, I would essentially be asking Him to choose another, makes my head hurt. Because when He *does* choose someone else and it *does* work—because it was always designed to work—and I see that person living in my promise, I promise you, I'mo be UBB-set.

I'm sure you've also experienced your own Mordecai Moment. It's that pivotal point where you're presented with a choice to either take God at His word and rise to the occasion of your calling, or be lulled to passivity through fear. If you're reading this book, chances are you've chosen wisely, or you're about to. When God asked me what else I had after my pageant prayer, it was a rhetorical question. He wasn't looking for an answer but was instead reminding me that there would be times when I wouldn't have anything—no backup plans, no resources, no good ideas—and I would still need to believe that I actually had everything I needed within me to play my position.

In Mordecai's final appeal to Esther, he suggested that perhaps the whole point of her becoming queen was for her to use her position for "such a time as this" (Est. 4:14 NIV).

A life of purpose is rarely one where you get to skate by unfazed, untested, or unchallenged.

That's my favorite part of the story, because it points to the bamboozle-ment of it all. Who knows, maybe Vashti *had* to act up so they could search for a new queen, and maybe Esther *had* to keep her identity a secret so she could be the one chosen, and maybe Haman *had* to stir up beef with the Jews so Esther would have some skin in the game and be in the best position to help.

Who knows?

For such a time as this, maybe that job had to let you go, because if not, you never would've started the business. Maybe you had to move cross-country because your small town would've limited your potential. Maybe you had to go through that breakup to gain clarity on what you truly desired. I don't pretend to know your backstory or even your front story, but I do know that God knows your final destination. And He can get you there a lot faster as soon as you relinquish control and abandon your own ideas of the best route to take. That's what Esther finally did. She came to her senses and decided to risk it all by approaching King Xerxes, declaring "If I perish, I perish" (Est. 4:16 NIV). What should've led to her death, actually became the turning point in their marriage. He put her love on top and spared her life after she revealed her true identity. The thing that Esther feared the most—rejection, divorce, death—was a nonissue after all. And when Xerxes got hip to Haman's scheming ways, he had him hanged, then pardoned the Jews, and gave Mordecai a job on his staff. Would'ya look at that. Because Esther was willing to play her position, even Uncle Mordi got on payroll at the palace. Talk about a come up!

With the pageant, I took a page out of Esther's book and gave God my very own "If I perish, I perish" declaration and agreed to perform-ing comedy. For two weeks, I was on high alert, searching for funny within the dual perspective of being both Nigerian and American. My only reference for comedy was when my brothers and I used to sneak into my parents' bedroom to watch *Def Comedy Jam* on HBO. I didn't know all the right technique, but Jesus never asks us to know everything before we start. He just asks us to get going. He'll give you what you need along the way.

While I performed, the audience laughed so much at my jokes that it kinda threw me off. I hadn't prepared to pause for laughter. I just wanted to plow through the experience and jump off the stage, so that was a surprise. After I'd finished, a reporter covering the event asked if I also performed at birthdays or weddings. Never one to pass up an opportunity, I quickly said, "Yup! And bar mitzvahs too!" Sometimes you gotta faith it 'til you make it! (See chapter 5.) Like Esther, through that single act of boldness, God provided the right people who would use their power, their ability, and their influence on my behalf. The makeup artist at the pageant (who wasn't Nigerian, but was married to one) enjoyed my set so much that she connected me with another one of her clients—a well-known comic in the DC area. Go figure.

Don't you miss out on your blessing because you're stuck between reason and logic. Everything in you might be shouting, *What if it doesn't work?*, but try switching perspectives for a hot second and focus instead on, *What if it does work?* More would be gained than lost, and not just for you, but for everyone connected to you.

> I don't pretend to know your backstory or even your front story, but I do know that God knows your final destination.

I honestly wish I had something more amazing about me that could take credit for the life I'm currently living, but all I've got is simply a by-product of an intense work ethic, blind faith, and the willingness to play my position and say, *"I don't know where we going, Jesus, but let's ride."* God's ability coupled with your availability can lead to infinite possibilities.

CHAPTER 3

GET'CHYA MIND RIGHT

When I was eleven, my mom took a hammer to my Lil' Kim CD. Drastic, I know. Considering that all she had to do to destroy the disc was to snap it in half or put a tiny scratch on the back to ensure endless skipping. But, nope, she needed to teach me a lesson, so hammer it was. *Hard Core* was only the second album I'd ever purchased on my own. (The first was Alanis Morissette's *Jagged Little Pill.* "You Oughta Know" is still my go-to karaoke song!) Every time I listened to the radio and heard Lil' Kim spit, "I Momma, Miss Ivana / Usually rock the Prada, sometimes Gabbana," I knew I had to cop the whole album. Sure, she was a little risqué and rapped about highly sexually explicit content. Yes, the album cover had her straddling a grizzly bear rug, staring suggestively at the camera. I'm aware that her music came with an "eighteen years or older" parental advisory warning and I was only eleven. Why else do you think I went through the trouble of having my older cousin buy it for me? *Duh!*

My mom worked long hours as a nurse at Howard University Hospital, so I knew to only play the album during the day, before she got home. What I hadn't anticipated was that, one day, my uncle would be making a random stop at the crib and would find the album booklet, showcasing Kim with her legs spread apart. I knew then that it was about to be a problem. He waited at our house for my mom to get home, evidence in hand, ready to be judge, jury, and executioner. One look at those images was enough for my mom to reach for the hammer and send my precious CD shattering into a million little pieces—proving that Lil' Kim wasn't the only hard-core person in our house.

Message received.

Or was it? I wasn't ready to accept defeat, but how was I going to outsmart the adults *and* get what I wanted? Remember earlier, when I said that the only thing Nigerians love more than education is *more* education? Well, I had my cousin buy me another copy of the album and I dubbed it onto a blank disc, which I labeled "Algebra Notes." My mom was none the wiser. It was a risky move, but I learned early on to have the mindset to use whatever I had—be it resources, intellect, or wit—to rise above any circumstance. That skill would prove useful as I embarked into the entertainment industry. Trust me, it wasn't always easy to maintain the right frame of mind in the face of countless rejections, but it was detrimental not to.

I remember trying to get work as a commercial actress, and my good friend Bechir connected me with his agent. This agent was well known and had lots of working clients. But before anyone could get an actual meeting with him, they had to do an on-camera audition with his assistant. If the agent liked what he saw, then he'd sign you on the spot. Well, I did the audition three times, and on three separate occasions, all I heard was crickets. After the first two tries, I came back filled with hope and optimism, but that third time was a blow to my ego. Soon, all the damaging thoughts I'd tried to suppress started swirling in my mind: *Maybe they were right. Maybe I'm just chasing pipe dreams. I guess I did miss my window. I can't even do stinking commercials; how did I think I was going to win an Oscar one day?*

To be clear, this is *not* the right mindset when facing challenging moments. It only leads to unproductivity, comparisons, and the desire to drink. We can't go around beating ourselves up. Not when we actually have a real-life adversary called the devil, who stays on his grind, using lies to steal, kill, and destroy our dreams, joy, and peace. He'd love nothing more than to see us fail, so let's not help him on his hustle.

A few days after my mental meltdown, Bechir spoke to the agent on my behalf, and he told me that before he could represent me, I'd need to take a specialized class and also change my hair color. Needless to say, I was pissed. I told Bechir that if this agent didn't want me, then he should've just said so instead of making me jump through all these stupid hoops for a "maybe." I felt like he was only stringing me along because Bechir was one of his top clients, and I personally didn't want to be anybody's charity case.

Thank God for the wisdom and patience of good friends who will steer you back on track when you're teetering on the edge of ridiculousness. Bechir insisted that I not major on the minor. He assured me that hair color wasn't

> We actually have a real-life adversary called the devil, who stays on his grind, using lies to steal, kill, and destroy our dreams, joy, and peace.

gon'stop me from being great, and suggested that if the agent hadn't seen any potential in me, he wouldn't have even wasted his time giving me pointers. He also reminded me that there were tons of aspiring actors who rarely get the luxury of feedback. They just mostly receive silence and go about never knowing how they could improve. Rather than getting upset, Bechir challenged me to look at the classes and the critique as an opportunity for growth.

He was right. I was being stubborn because I wanted a win so bad. I wanted to prove to everyone who doubted my success that they were wrong and that I was indeed capable of making my dreams come true. But that was a futile mission. I mean, why waste your time trying to prove yourself to the "theys" and the "thems," when you're doing something *they* can't do? What I really needed to do was shatter the need to gain everyone's approval like my mom shattered my Lil' Kim CD. Some habits can't simply be scratched on the surface. You gotta take a hammer to those heauxz, so they can be completely demolished.

I swallowed my pride and took the agent's advice, and after three months of training, he signed me as a commercial client, and I went on to book a national television campaign. Turns out, I had the goods already in me. My mind and skills just needed to be fine-tuned.

I'm sure Joshua, in Da Good Book, felt the same way. After Moses died, God told his assistant, Josh, to stop crying about it and get to work 'cuz he was in charge of the Israelites now. If you understood the gravity of the situation, you'd know that sometimes, God be wildin'. Moses was the LeBron of Israel. He was the one God enabled to sweep the Egyptians in a playoff of plagues, part the Red Sea, and lead the Israelites to the freedom Olympics. *That's* whose shoes Joshua was supposed to fill?

God clearly knew He was asking a tall order, because in His pep talk that lasted nine verses, He stressed for Joshua to be "strong and courageous." He repeated this three times, and what's funny is that Joshua never said a word. Usually when you repeat yourself that many times, it's because the other person keeps interrupting. But nope, Josh was just listening. I imagine God heard Joshua's unspoken fear. He saw the hidden anxiety. He felt the trepidation, and He knew that despite all the promises He made, like, *"I will never leave you nor forsake you. As I was with Moses, so I will be with you. You will be prosperous and very successful,"* if Joshua's mind wasn't right, none of them would matter.

What unspoken fears haven't you dared utter? Are there promises God keeps speaking to you that you can't hear over the banging of doubt? How many times will He have to tell *you* to be strong and courageous before it seeps into your psyche that you can do hard things too? What I think is dope is that God's confidence in Joshua became contagious. When Josh told the Israelites the plan of action that God gave him, they didn't panic. They didn't have a vote of no confidence because their beloved leader was replaced by his water boy. Nope. They received Joshua with these reassuring words: "Whatever you have commanded us we will do and wherever you send us, we will go.... Only be strong and courageous!"[1]

How did they know to reaffirm God's words back to Joshua? And why did they add *"only"*? Was it because there were other options for him to be,

> *Why waste your time trying to prove yourself to the "theys" and the "thems," when you're doing something they can't do?*

1. Joshua 1:16–18 NIV.

so they needed to simplify his choices? In your case, is God telling you to *only* be fearless and confident in pursuing that degree? Is He stressing for you to *only* be dedicated and persistent in starting that new endeavor? Perhaps He's encouraging you to *only* be trusting and hopeful in believing that you *will* find companionship. Whatever it is, this is your opportunity to get it together. The rapper Memphis Bleek had a song that went, "I got my mind right, money right, ready for war," and the reality is, there's a battlefield over your thoughts. You gotta fight to get'chya mind right so your faith can stay in check.

When Joshua finally took the reins of his purpose, the help he needed showed up. The strength he required was developed. The strategy, support, and favor that were essential to his success were divinely provided. If you're thinking, *Well, that's great that Joshua got all those people to back him up. I wish I had that level of support,* let me remind you that long before anybody agreed to follow Joshua on Instagram or in real life, God gave him the assurance that He would be with him, just like He'd been with Moses. And if you know anything about math (other than it's a great decoy on blank CDs), then you know that You + God = a majority. With Him on your team, you can't lose—but'chyu actually gotta believe that.

You're definitely gonna face harsh critics and tough situations. Circumstances will feel out of your control. Problems will appear more powerful than your abilities. That's a fact, but the Truth of God's Word trumps a fact on any day of every week. While your situation is working hard to throw you off, your mind has to be equally as vigilant in reminding you of the things

You + God = a majority.

that make you worthy of your calling. I don't care if it's as basic as reciting the affirmations Viola Davis's character said to the little girl in the movie *The Help*: "You is smart. You is kind. You is important." Or if it's as detailed as the mantra I declare when facing a battle: "I'm dangerous to the enemy's camp. If I wasn't, he wouldn't be this pressed to see me fall. There's something great in my life that makes him tremble, that's why he's attacking me from every angle. But I've been genetically predisposed to foil all his plans, so I can't give up so easily!"

Whatever you choose, say it boldly and say it often. That's how you renew your mind like Da Good Book suggests in Romans 12:3. You exchange losing with thoughts of winning. You trade in barely enough with believing for more. You swap out hopelessness for a blessed assurance. The reality is, we've all been designed for greatness, because God Himself is great. And if God lives in us, then our default factory setting is to also be great.

Years after booking those commercials, my mindset would once again be tested when I auditioned for the role of Molly on *Insecure*. I went through several rounds of auditions—five to be exact (I detail the entire experience in chapter 14). A year after the show premiered, our showrunner, Prentice Penny, found the casting notes he'd made about my initial performance. He was very honest in sharing that I didn't have the best first audition. There was another actress who'd knocked it out of the park and was actually their first choice. How's that for a reminder to stay humble?

> *If God lives in us, then our default factory setting is to also be great.*

But in all honesty, that actress very well should've been. I was as green as a Trader Joe's avocado. It was my first time trying out for such a high-caliber role, and without much experience, I had to rely heavily on natural instincts and the sheer belief that God's got me. Thankfully, it all paid off. Prentice noted that with each subsequent audition, I kept improving, whereas the favored actress peaked where she started. Between each audition, I never let myself rest on the laurels of what I'd done right the time before. I found new ways to interpret the scenes, and I took risks like prioritizing getting a private coach for an hour over paying my cell-phone bill that month.

My growth in each audition led the producers to believe that if I could show this much progress on my own, then there was no telling how much better I could be when given actual direction. On the surface, my limited expertise should've taken me out of the running, but the thing that makes you qualified is not always visible. It's incubated in your thoughts, it's developed in your words, and cultivated in your willingness to envision yourself the way God does.

At a leadership conference put on by Curlbox CEO and homie Myleik Teele, she gave out journals that said "I'm the magic" inscribed on the cover. As I mentioned earlier, I struggled for some time to realize what my magic was. I would often downplay or discredit the things that made me truly valuable with the misconception that "anyone could do that." I was shocked to discover that everybody *doesn't* do things like I do, or see things the way I see them. I've since learned that my ability to encourage others, connect random dots, pay super close attention to the minutest details, and cultivate relationships are just a few examples of my Black girl magic at work. Those specific observations and nuances about myself are what make me the visionary for my calling. You have to discover your own special sauce, and once you do, never dilute it. What they don't tell you is that the unwatered-down version of you is 'bout to be a hot commodity.

When we tap into our most authentic selves, we have an opportunity to be the thing people didn't even know they were looking for, but now can't live without. I know it gets hard to believe that what you have to offer will be widely accepted, especially when there are so many others in the game who are just as good, or even better. But don't allow yourself to be defeated before you even get started.

Your supply is so necessary. First Corinthians confirms that by highlighting how certain features of your body can't deem themselves as insignificant because they don't measure up to other features. The ear can't disqualify itself because it isn't an eye, any more than the foot can dismiss itself because it's not a hand. Without feet, we wouldn't have red bottoms—and what kind of life is that!

You are indispensable.

Full stop. Period. The end.

When you start wondering how someone like you—from the family you're from, the city you live in, with the tough breaks you've had, and the money you don't have   could dream this improbable dream, remind yourself to only be strong and courageous. And if you need reinforcements for when the discouragement creeps in, make your way to your local grocery store. One stroll down the water aisle and you should feel the inspiration rising. Trust me on this. All the options on display

The unwatered-down version of you is 'bout to be a hot commodity.

started with a single thought. Someone saw H$_2$O and thought, *Yeah, that's great, but that's mineral water. Mountain water tastes so much better.* Then somebody else came after that and decided that spring water was where it was at. It didn't stop there. Somehow we got flavored water and sparkling water and even alkaline water.

In the same vein, don't allow yourself to disqualify what you bring to the table just because someone else sat down before you. Who cares if your meal is still baking? There's a seat with your name on it. Today, God wants to give you a blank disc. He's erasing every thought that He never programmed in you and dubbing His original purpose back into you. He's taking a Sharpie and rewriting your history. Where others have called you hopeless, He's labeled you redeemed. They may accuse you, but He calls you forgiven. They'll say you're not lovable, smart, important, or rich, but His titles for you are friend, chosen, and blessed. So get'chya mind right and go be great.

CHAPTER 4

I SAID IT,
I MEANT IT,
I'M HERE TO
REPRESENT IT!

It's not only important to know *who* you are, but equally as important to know *whose* you are. Who I am is determined, fun-loving, and optimistic. Whose I am is Mike and Celine's daughter. There are some risks I can't afford to take because of who my parents are—like the time in seventh grade when I got into a fight. Well, it wasn't really much of a fight. I let the girl punch me in the face and then promptly reported her. It's not that I didn't want to fight back, I just thought too much about the consequences and the chain reaction that would follow. Had I retaliated, we *both* would've gotten suspended off the bus, which would've added unnecessary financial stress on my mom, 'cuz she would've had to take time off from work to make sure I got to school safely. I can't be out here messin' up my momma's money. But not a day goes by where I don't think about how I should've popped that girl in her throat. I guess, like my Forever First Lady, Michelle Obama, said, when they go low, we go high…or whateva.

But being a part of the Orji family comes with its own set of perks. For instance, whenever my family would return to Nigeria and go to my grandfather's compound in the village, we were assured two things: (1) we would be treated with honor and respect, and (2) the villagers would prepare a feast for us. That's 'cuz my grandfather was the king, or the Ogbuefi, of our village and my dad, a titled chief. While it's cool that my grandaddy was a king, what's even more dope is that you and I belong to a family where our Heavenly Father is the King of Kings.

Knowing whose we are in our relationship with God should empower us with an unshakable confidence that settles every matter. Personally, it gives me the audacity to hope and the tenacity to dare people to come against what's rightfully mine. I may have been apprehensive to fight as a kid, but now I know that whose I am affords me backup from a host of Heavenly angels, ready and willing to show up on the scene and handle my light work.

I don't know about'chyu, but I love a good testimony. Other people may get jealous from them, but I get inspired. They remind me that if God can come through for others, then He can make things shake for me. Obviously, my breakthroughs will happen differently, but the endless possibilities get my faith fired up. Here's a good testimony for you. When I first moved to LA, it became evident that I needed a car in the worst way. Unlike New York, Los Angeles doesn't have a sophisticated subway system. It can take hours to get around town on public transport (honestly, it can also take hours to get down the street in a car, but at least it smells nicer and you can control the music).

I applied for a job as a production assistant, even though it required me to have a vehicle, which I. Did. Not. But by the grace of God (and a solid résumé, with a good recommendation), they hired me anyway. My commute to work took an hour, spent on two buses. When my bosses needed me to run an errand, I'd use their car or they'd rent me one. After a few months, the job ended, and I found myself back in need of wheels.

I remembered that several months earlier, a young lady told me that someone she didn't even know had given her one of their extra cars. I particularly enjoyed this testimony because, at the time, I couldn't fathom where one had to be in their lives financially to *give* away a car. *For free.* Not sell to make a profit. I aspired to such levels of generosity where I could bless someone out of the abundance of my overflow. However, in *that* moment, I desperately needed God to work a similar miracle on my behalf.

I called the woman to hear her car-giving testimony again, and she shared that she'd since gotten rid of the car and had leased one of her own. She even offered me her dealer's information and insisted that I contact him for a good deal. Not exactly what I was expecting to hear, but as soon as I hung up, I heard *"God say, Go buy a car."* There He goes again talking reckless. When I *had* a job, I was taking the bus. But when I'm unemployed, *that's* when God wants me to go to the dealership and buy a car? WITH WHAT MONEY, SWAY? Huh? Like an Avril Lavigne song, why Jesus gotta go and make things so complicated? But I knew my faith was being stretched. God was purposely using a desperate situation to let me know that if He said it, He meant it, and He was gonna represent it!

I called the dealer and they sent an employee to pick me up. While riding shotgun, I turned to the driver and told him, with all the confidence in the world, "You might be picking me up now, but I'll be driving myself home tonight." I had no idea how God was going to make it happen, but with my words, I was releasing my angels to get crackin'. Some of your angels are bored to death waiting on standby. They're full of everything but handcuffed to nothing, because you haven't activated their potential. All I gave mine to work with was a belief that zero dollars, an amazing credit score, and a low-limit credit card would be enough to drive me off the lot. When the author in Isaiah 55:1 said, "You who have no money, come, buy..." (NIV) he was clearly talking about me.

In the past, my family had gotten all of our cars from auctions (because: immigrant), so I didn't know how an actual dealership worked. I figured I'd have to play hardball, and being Nigerian, haggling is like an Olympic sport for me. Five thousand dollars was my max budget and I didn't want a monthly note that exceeded $150. Those parameters took leasing off the table and limited me to preowned vehicles. What had worked for my friend wouldn't work for me, and that's okay, because her testimony was good enough to get me in the door. I'm certain the dealer thought I was coo-coo for Cocoa Puffs for coming through with no funds and the audacity to have a wish list.

Clearly, he didn't understand the difference between who I was and *whose* I was. As we walked around, I saw a used 2001 Honda Accord that was in great condition, but had a sticker price of $7,500. I really wanted the car, but I wasn't

Some of your angels are bored to death waiting on standby.

prepared to go above my $5,000 limit. The sales agent crunched all the numbers and even brought in reinforcements to try to convince me that it was a good deal, but I told him that if we couldn't get closer to my terms, then I'd just have to go somewhere else.

Y'all, there wasn't somewhere else to go. I was just high off the confidence of a spoken word from Jesus. After several hours of haggling, test driving, and form filling, the girl with no job and no money ended up getting the car for $5,500 with monthly payments of $172. The mechanics who serviced the cars on the lot told me to drive away quickly before they changed their minds, 'cuz I'd just practically stolen the car. Exactly like I said I would, I drove myself home that night, because once God settles a thing, it *has* to happen. Sure, some months were a stretch, and at times I had to delay a payment or two when things got really tight. But in those moments when God didn't change the situation, He altered how I *reacted* to it. Instead of trippin' out, I reminded myself that while I might be taking a hit, it wouldn't be like this always. And it wasn't.

Four years after I bought the car, my career took off and I was able to upgrade to a luxury lease. Instead of trading in the Honda, I paid off the balance and gave it away as a gift to my good friend Hari. The very thing I had wanted someone to do for me, God made possible for me to do for someone else. That's how getting bamboozled by Jesus happens. I needed to hear a testimony, but God turned me into one.

In Da Good Book, God turned a little guy named David into a walking testimony as well. If you're familiar with the David and Goliath story, then you know that David was a celebrated war hero, whose claim to fame was taking down the giant Goliath. But that's only half the story. To fully appreciate what led to David's defining moment, you gotta peel back the layers and dig a little deeper. For starters, David was the youngest of eight sons. He was disliked by his brothers and forgotten by his father. A lowly shepherd boy, he was handsome but short. Nevertheless, David was fully convinced that despite *who* he was, *whose* he was as a child of God would always carry more weight.

> *I needed to hear a testimony, but God turned me into one.*

That's why when he showed up on the battlefield and saw how the Philistine giant, Goliath, was talking crazy to the Israelite army, he got downright indignant. How dare someone as unworthy as Goliath use his mouth to disrespect God's people and still have all his teeth? Someone had to shut him up, and David volunteered himself as tribute. What separated him from all the other soldiers who were too shook to battle Goliath was his unshakable belief that if God be for him, no giant could stop him.

That's the same belief that'll separate you from other students who won't get the scholarship. Sure, you're all smart, but you have an advantage that intellect alone can't penetrate. It's also what'll separate you from all your single friends who are convinced that there are no more good men or women left in the world. I personally know that can't be true 'cuz I'm still single, so there's gotta be at least ONE good guy left, and he's got my name tatted all over him—so back off!

Not everyone will be a fan of your convictions, but don't let that stop you from having them. One of David's own brothers overheard him inquiring about fighting Goliath and felt the need to put him in his place. Keep in mind that this was the same brother who was too scared to face Goliath himself. Whenever you tap into whose you are, someone is bound to be mad that you dared to do what they couldn't, but you can't be responsible for their insecurities and shortcomings. That's what therapy is for. David might've been young and short, but he was nobody's punk. He responded to his brother by turning away. That turn-away is key. When folks start yappin' at the mouth and get out of pocket, hit 'em with a David, and turn all the way away.

With his back to those who didn't have his back, David told King Saul (not to be confused with the Saul who later became the Apostle Paul) that he would fight Goliath. But just like David's brother, the king tried to box David in by telling him all the reasons why his plan would fail. For starters, he felt that David was too inexperienced in battle, but that wasn't true at all. Sure, Goliath had been a killa since birth, but David's résumé was nothing to laugh at. In the past, he'd protected his daddy's sheep from lions and tigers and bears (oh my), so he figured Goliath could catch those same hands.

You'll face giants that look new, but don't believe the hype. You've seen them before. They might be packaged differently, but that's 'cuz the devil ain't got new tricks. He's just repurposing the same ol' darts to throw your way, hoping something sticks. When the attacks come, think back on all your past wins and apply them to your current troubles. Soon enough, your tests will become your testimony.

I know it sucks to have to keep fighting battles over and over again, but those tough breaks aren't meant to exhaust you. They're a training camp to help you face the Goliaths in your life. When you realize that you're not fighting from the strength of your muscles, but from the strength of your faith, it tips the scales of winning in your favor.

When King Saul finally agreed to let David fight, he tried to give him an edge by putting his very expensive, stately armor on him, but the way David was set up, he couldn't handle all that weight. It was too restrictive. We've all been burdened by the weight of somebody else's armor. Maybe that looks like putting on a career, a thought pattern, or advice that just doesn't fit. Just because your momma was married and had three babies by the time she was your age doesn't mean that's the will of God for your life. And just because your daddy did such and such at so and so doesn't mean that's what you were destined to do too. Sure, you might come from a long line of [insert profession here], but you can be the one to start a new line.

Da Good Book insists that we strip off every unnecessary weight that keeps us entangled in useless patterns, and urges us to run our own race. Which is exactly what David did. He took off that heavy artillery and went with what he knew best: five measly stones powered by faith and a sure shot. What Saul saw as a toy in David's hand, David saw as an opportunity to make God's name famous. Don't worry that your wins won't occur the way others might imagine. They'll happen the way God intended. So be fully satisfied with what works for you.

> You'll face giants that look new, but don't believe the hype. You've seen them before.

Sure, someone else could have bigger and flashier resources, but bigger and flashier doesn't always mean better and more helpful. God will use what He's given you, as insignificant as it seems, to be exactly what's needed to take you higher.

Some of y'all are being slowed down now, 'cuz you're wearing sneakers to a situation that God told you to put on slippers for. Take 'em off! It might not make a whole lotta'sense to a whole lotta'people, it may look a little messier. Heck, it might even take a little while longer, but that's what sets your journey apart. Everything God put *in* you has equipped you for the battle and everything God is *to* you has prepared you to succeed. He set it up that way, and will do everything in His power to defend it.

CHAPTER 5

FAITH IT 'TIL
YOU MAKE IT

To make extra money as a comic, I began hosting anything with a microphone—weddings, baby showers, funerals. You name it, and I was probably the ultimate hype-woman at the event. Unfortunately, it's easy for customers to take advantage of you when you're an entrepreneur with a staff of one. Clients were always asking for more, while offering to pay less. To avoid this pesky little issue, I got me an assistant. And by "assistant," I mean, created a Google Voice number and made up an alias. "Kristen" began running point on scheduling meetings, making travel arrangements, and processing payments between "Ms. Orji" and all clients. Nothing brought me more pleasure than getting to say, *My assistant handles that. I'll put you two in touch via email.* Hey, you gotta faith it 'til you make it! Six years after the creation of "Kristen," I was able to hire my first (real-life) full-time assistant.

"Faith'n it" requires you to operate from a place where your problems are already solved, even though they're staring you dead in the face. It doesn't mean you're in *denial* about them—that would be fakin' it. But it does mean that you're choosing to believe for better *despite* your circumstances.

I can't e'en front, though, faith'n it got me played when I first moved to New York in 2009. Apparently, I wasn't hip to all the rules of comedy when I arrived. I thought all you had to do to get stage time was be funny, and then once you got noticed, BOOM: You'd get your big break and transition to acting.

False.

I got turned down and told "no" so often, you would'a thought I was a guy at a club tryna get the City's number. The biggest scam I ran into were "bringer" shows. That's where a comic had to bring at least five friends, each paying a full-price ticket and ordering a two-drink minimum in order to perform at mainstream clubs. Talk about how to lose friends and alienate people! Being that I only brought myself to New York, that lil' setup wasn't gon' work for me, but how was I supposed to get my practice on?

One day, I attended an open mic, which is more like a comedy focus group—you're able to hone new material in front of an audience, but that audience is composed mostly of comics who are solely focused on their own sets. The host announced that he needed a replacement to run the weekly spot. I waited for one of the many guys in the room to jump at the chance, but no one did, so I volunteered myself. What

> *"Faith'n it" requires you to operate from a place where your problems are already solved, even though they're staring you dead in the face.*

the other comics saw as unwanted responsibility, I saw as divine opportunity. I figured that if I was the host of my own comedy show, then I would have the power to give other comics stage time and cut through all the red tape of performing. There was one small hiccup, though: I didn't know anything about running a room.

That's the essence of faith'n it 'til you make it. It requires you to jump in head first, knowing you can't swim, but trusting that God will provide a life raft. I might not have known what I was doing, but I knew someone who did. I called up a guy in DC who ran the open mic I used to frequent, and he gave me practical advice on how to advertise, the right equipment to purchase, and even how to make it a fun experience so I could attract an audience that wasn't 90 percent comics. I named the show *Momma, I Made It!* (MiMi), because I couldn't wait for the day when I could actually call home and utter those words.

I was working as a temp at the time, so after paying rent, I used the leftover money to buy an amplifier, lights, and all the other fixings to make it feel like a real comedy club experience. Was it fun dragging all that equipment on the subway from Harlem to Midtown every week? Not at all. Were there nights I felt like canceling the show because I was too tired to muster up the strength to laugh? Absolutely. In the beginning, was it discouraging that after giving it my all, we still only had three people in the audience? Heck yeah. But rising to the challenge of running MiMi prepared me to spearhead my very first multi-city, Lagos to Laurel comedy tour, over a decade later.

Creating a professional experience at that open mic showed me that I cared more about excellence than ease. Setting out a room full of chairs when we averaged a handful of guests taught me that I had vision beyond sight. Gaining favor with the owner of the venue, who didn't charge us to utilize the space, revealed that God will offer unlimited provision when I display unparalleled faith. Not only did MiMi help me grow as a performer, it also positioned me to meet a slew of talented comics who've gone on to achieve tremendous success—many of whom I'm still fortunate to call friends today. It was only fitting then that, when I went on to write, executive produce, and star in my very own HBO comedy special in 2020, I also titled it *Momma, I Made It!*

Some of your biggest blessings won't appear like the bright, glaring Krispy Kreme "Hot Now" sign. They'll come wrapped as a beautiful burden. They'll look like a hurdle, feel like a chore, and will probably come at the most inopportune time. But before you say EFFF it, consider saying *F*-it, and by that, I mean faith it. That's what Jesus' momma did. One day, she accompanied Jesus and His disciples to a wedding reception where the bottles were poppin' and the good times were flowing. Eventually, the wine ran out, and when Mary went to tell Jesus, He looked at her sideways and said, "Woman, what that gotta do with me?"

God will offer unlimited provision when I display unparalleled faith.

Now, I know there's a lot of speculation about Jesus' race, but I think this verse has proven, once and for all, that Jesus was in fact mixed. 'Cause no 100 percent Black kid could'a called his momma "woman" and not get popped in the throat. I'm just saying.

Anyway, when Jesus bucked at Mary about the wine, she didn't even flinch. She walked away quietly, went straight to the servants, and said, "Do whatever he tells you to do."[1] That's quintessential faith'n it 'til you make it, right there. She had no idea what the outcome would be, but she understood that He was Jesus, so the possibilities were endless. He told the workers to fill up some jars with water, and as they served it to the guests, it miraculously turned to wine.

We happen to have the unfair advantage of knowing how that story ends, but in real time, think about how scared those servants must've been. When folks are expecting wine and you're carrying them a glass filled with water, that takes some next-level faith to trust that Jesus could turn it in time, before it hit their lips. And real talk, they didn't even know turning it was an option. All they knew was that Mary knew something they didn't. And if His own momma wasn't trippin', then who were they to panic?

Believing is key to faith'n it, 'cuz it unlocks the blessing. One of my favorite passages of Scripture says, "Blessed is she who has believed that the Lord would fulfill his promises to her."[2] It doesn't say, "Blessed is she who has done the most," or "Blessed is she who wrote a business plan." Nah, it just says, "Blessed is she who *believed*." That means that your belief and your blessing go together like chicken and waffles. However, don't think that just 'cuz you're out here believing, that means that you don't have to do any of the work. Remember, the servants still had to fill the jars and still had to serve the drinks. That's work. Unfortunately, too many people who wear the label "Christian" believe that title exempts them from taking initiative and gettin' down and dirty. Faith without works is a dead-end street, but believing is the juice that turns the streetlights on.

---

1. John 2:1–5 NIV.
2. Luke 1:45 NIV.

I can't call how long you're gonna need to be believing before you see your blessing, but I can tell you that there's no such thing as an "overnight success." For a lot of folks, it was a series of veeeeeeerry long nights. It took me seven years to be discovered, and one of the most important things I learned in that season is that success is created when strife has been perfected. I know it sounds ridiculous, but your struggles are a gift. Matter of fact, Da Good Book encourages us to *consider* it a sheer gift when challenges come at us from all sides. That kind of pressure forces our faith life into the open and exposes its true colors. We actually would be doing ourselves a disservice to quit prematurely in the middle of tough times. Our job is to let patience marinate in us so we don't become half-baked in faith.[3]

I definitely had to stew in some tests to let them develop my faith, and trust me, nothing about that was sexy. I'll never forget the night I wanted to head into Manhattan to grab a slice of pizza. Not having a lot of cash to work with in those days, my favorite pizza spot became 2 Bros Pizza. You could get two slices and a drink for $2.75. I used to joke that with those prices, they fed both the artists and the homeless. When I pulled together all the money I had to my name, I couldn't even come up with $7.75 for a roundtrip subway fare *and* food. Here I was, twenty-five years old with a master's degree, and was struggling to find loose change.

Starving and angry, I contemplated going to the kitchen and making a syrup sandwich, which ain't nothing but a poor man's French toast—with more toast than French. I was tired of the struggle meal. I wanted something hot that felt like cooked food. I deserved at least *that* much at this point in my life. As I sat in bed and felt the warm tears

3. See James 1:2–4.

roll down my cheeks, I felt Holy Spirit tryna speak, but I didn't know if I wanted to hear it.

Not being a *complete* idiot, I grabbed my pen and paper and waited, because when Spirit speaks, you take copious notes. What followed next was a God-led download, a dissertation that filled an entire page. It was a dissertation of promised blessings that still serves as my blueprint of faith to this very day. In one of my darkest hours, God gave me a hope that seemed both glorious and insurmountable. His promises felt exciting, yet cruel. Here He was, telling me how I would experience immense success, but all I could see was everything I lacked.

I read those lofty promises and thought, *Yeah, this sounds real good, Jesus, but I don't need all'a that right now. Just gimme two cheese slices and a grape Fanta!* There was a tug-of-war between the blind belief Jesus required of me and the visible strife eating away at my esophagus. When what you physically see appears more real than what God is trying to show you, there will always be conflict in your spirit. This is the conundrum that makes faith'n it 'til you make it so difficult. But know this, when hard times come, and they will, all you gotta do is outlast your darkest night by one day, and you win. Yes, you might be hard pressed on every side, but you're not crushed; perplexed, but not in despair; persecuted, but not abandoned; struck down, but still not destroyed. You got this.

> All you gotta do is outlast your darkest night by one day, and you win.

With hunger pains piercing my side, I knew that worrying wasn't gonna get me fed. My tears couldn't quench my thirst. The only logical thing to do was call it a night and hope for a better tomorrow. And better it was. The next morning, I woke up to the sweet smell of breakfast and was greeted to a plate of pancakes, eggs, and bacon. Jacque, the woman I was staying with, had made a feast, and I couldn't help but wonder if God had whispered my needs in her ears as she slept.

It was September 2009 when God deposited those words into my spirit, and for over a decade, I've kept that sheet of paper tucked in my Bible, pulling it out every so often to verify the manifestation of a promise. It's blown my mind to see things I'd written actually show up exactly how Jesus said they would. And when they didn't, I'd tell myself, *Nah, boo, that ain't it. Keep going 'til you see what it says.* It's certainly been a process, but I've learned that when we rush the process or don't trust the roller coaster, when we give up too soon, or refuse to even try, we choke the umbilical cord attached to our purpose and ultimately destroy, delay, or downgrade our destinies. Kinda' like how Abraham did, earning him the title as the first F-boy to ever exist.

God had personally promised Abraham that he would have an heir, but Abe still wasn't convinced. He was getting old, and his wife, Sarah, wasn't exactly a spring chicken. In his impatience, Abe bypassed what God said and took matters into his own hands. Sarah had a maid named Hagar, and in the first-ever account of an open marriage, she gave Abraham permission to do da nasty with her. Hagar was hecka fertile, so of course, she became pregnant emeejiatly. Sarah got all up in her feelings and demanded that Abraham make Hagar exit stage left. This is when Abraham reached F-boy status. I know you want to picture him differently, but all the signs are there: He slept with another woman while he was still married. Got said woman pregnant, and promptly sent her packing, 'cuz *she* was causing confusion in his marriage. I feel madd triggered right now.

No matter how long it takes to get what God's promised, don't confuse a delay with a denial and try to MacGyver your own come up. That only makes the situation worse. When God orchestrates a thing, He's the one responsible for the upkeep like AppleCare. Fourteen years after the debacle with Hagar, when Abraham was a hundred and Sarah, ninety, God made good on His word, and they had a son of their own. But look at all the chaos they created by heauxzing the process. Hagar became a single mother on welfare and her son, Ishmael, was left crying out, "*Why don't he love me, man?!*" like Will Smith to Uncle Phil in that iconic *Fresh Prince* episode where his daddy disappeared.

I know it's easy to get discouraged by how much older you're getting, but God is the author of time. He can daylight-savings you right to where you're supposed to be. In Isaiah, it says that God is in our lives from the very beginning, letting us in on what's to come, and assuring us that He's in this for the long haul.[4] Basically, God's already gone to the end of your life, retraced His steps, and mapped out every route along the way to get you to where He wants you. He knows every speed bump, detour, road closure, and pothole you'll ever hit, and navigates you to safety like a celestial GPS, so don't trip. Your faith isn't activated by perfect whining. It's manifested in God's perfect timing. It might feel like He's forgotten about you, but your feelings are like that shady uncle at the family reunion—they can't always be trusted.

> Don't confuse a delay with a denial.

---

4. See Isaiah 46:8–11.

CHAPTER 6

PRESSURE BURSTS PIPES, BUT ALSO MAKES DIAMONDS

'm not one to be motivated by peer pressure. I hate facing negative consequences way more than I desire to fit in. Growing up, my brothers would sneak into movie theaters, and I promised not to tell the parentals as long as they brought me a bag of peanut M&M's and peach gummics. They almost always forgot, and I almost always snitched. Clown me if you want, but they literally had *one* job! Recently, I was on a date, and after we'd finished watching the movie we'd paid for, we decided to see another one, which happened to be playing across the hall. He asked if I wanted to sneak in, and my childhood memories flooded me. This was my chance to finally be a rebel, so I decided to go for it. I went as far as sitting down in the mostly empty theater. But two minutes in, my integrity just couldn't stomach the pressure of getting caught. So we left, bought new tickets for the movie, and returned to our seats.

Similarly, your points of pressure reveal your strengths and weaknesses, and also form the catalyst for change in your life. To make a diamond from carbon atoms, you need three essential ingredients: heat, time, and pressure. Talk about a metaphor for our lives. When the heat gets turned up and the pressure piles on, only time will tell if you'll panic and crumble, or rise above the mayhem to shine bright like a diamond.

About a year before I booked *Insecure*, I experienced one of those diamond-making pressured points—only it came in the form of a soul-crushing career disappointment. There was a production company who'd approached me with the prospect of hosting my own talk show. Considering that it's long been a dream of mine to do so, I was geeked. I immediately started planning out my roster of guests. There were a lot of up-and-coming entrepreneurs, whose businesses I wanted to promote on my newly minted platform. My motto was, and still is, "When one eats, we all eat."

I didn't have any representation at the time who could look over the deal, so I called in a favor from my best friend, Rita, who's also a lawyer. She agreed to review the paperwork, but weeks went by and still no contract. However, the production company was steadily hitting me up to recommend talent for other projects they were working on. Not one to block anybody's blessings, I suggested a few names. I didn't think anything of it because what's mine is mine and can't nobody take it from me. Still, each time I would ask about *my* contract, they would lollygag with one excuse after another.

By now, you're well aware of the financial state I was in at the time. I was barely surviving from gig to gig, so the potential income I stood to gain from this opportunity would be a game changer. My patience and resilience were being tested like Jesus after fasting forty days and forty nights. That's a different kinda diet. Y'all thought the Whole 30 was bad, but Ya Boy was on that Insufficient 40! Homie wasn't hungry. He was hangry. After enduring that kind of pressure, you'd expect Jesus' first order of business to be a T-bone steak, but nope, He was bamboozled into being tempted by the devil.

Off rip, the enemy started taunting Jesus. He baited Him by questioning the essence of His character, talkin'bout, "If You're *really* the Son of God, I dare You to turn these stones into bread." That's triflin'. He knew Jesus was desperate for food and he was preying on His weakness. But that's exactly what this production company was doing with me. They *kneeew* I was famished financially and hungry for an opportunity. That's why they kept baiting me to see if my desperation would cause me to cave and accept whatever terms they offered.

I heard through the grapevine that they'd given someone else I'd recommended a nice-sized contract, so I set my expectations accordingly. When they finally came back with my rate, it was so low that it was borderline disrespectful. As if that wasn't bad enough, they also wanted to own my name and likeness. I didn't need Rita's expertise to see how terrible those terms were. The nothing I had was still better than the little they offered. At least my nothing still had my dignity attached, so I declined the job.

That setback nearly took me out and almost had me giving up. But after a few months, I came to myself, and learned to turn my pain into power. My annoyance became gasoline, and once lit, it sparked a

What's mine is mine and can't nobody take it from me.

drive so intense that I almost didn't recognize myself. By the following year, not only was I pitching my own show, but I'd also booked the role on *Insecure*. Of course, when that happened, those same producers tried to wiggle their way back into my life. They invited me to their studio to show off their new facility and tried to sell me on why they were the best execs to bring my show to life. Fool me once, shame on you. Fool me twice—stab yaself.

I let them roll out the red carpet and I marveled at how magnificent their amnesia was. I relished the opportunity to finally look them in the eyes and tell them I wasn't interested in partnering with them. They might've underestimated me before, but thanks to the pressure they'd applied, I was forced to flex my creativity in new and untapped ways.

One of the most accurate depictions of success comes from General George Patton. He said that "success is how high you bounce when you hit bottom," and I couldn't agree more. I've fallen to the bottom. I've felt the spring of that bounce. I've gone through agony to get to destiny, so, I know. That's why it brings me joy when my friends hit rock bottom. Not because of cruel intentions, but because it means they're about to experience their own bounce back. When they get sick and tired of being sick and tired of their present predicament, it unleashes the beast within. They're finally ready to discard logic, suspend reason, and go balls to the wall to give it their most uncomfortable and valiant effort.

I'm sure you've heard the saying, "If you can't stand the heat, then get up out the kitchen." While that makes for catchy rap lyrics, I totally disagree. When situations get too hot to handle, that's when you need to sit in the displeasure, push past the pain, and allow it to produce a stronger, better version of yourself. Now, if you're getting abused or violated, then yeah, get up on outta there, boo, 'cuz that ain't the will of Jesus for your life.

God often tests our faith under fire like He did with Dem Three Hebrew Boyz: Shadrach, Meshach, and A-Baaad-Negro, I mean, Abednego. As the story goes, King Nebuchadnezzar made it mandatory for everyone who heard his theme song to bow down and worship his golden statue. But Shadrach & Friends weren't about that life. They made it clear that they only bent a knee to the one true King of the North, God the Father. Well, Nebuchadnezzar didn't appreciate that. He went all Beyoncé on them, like, "You must not know 'bout me!" and threatened to throw them into a fire-blazing furnace if they didn't follow his instructions.

It's a lot of pressure to stand up for your beliefs in an environment that isn't conducive to them. For Shadrach and his homies, living their faith out loud could've literally cost them their lives, but they weren't fazed. They maintained their position, and even challenged Nebuchadnezzar, saying, "Listen here, Mr. King, you go ahead and do what'chyu feel is necessary, but as for me and my boys, we gon'serve our God, and He's gon'rescue us from whatever blaze you set. And even if you change your mind and don't kill us, we're *still* not gonna worship you and your stupid idols."[1] Dem Boyz must've been listening to "Knuck If You Buck" during praise and worship, 'cuz they were amped. They knew who they were, and firmly trusted in whose they were, and no matter how much pressure was applied to their situation, they weren't gonna get caught slippin'.

The king, on the other hand, was feeling tighter than a scrunchie. To make an example of the blatant disrespect to his authority, he ordered

1. See Daniel 3:8–18.

the furnace turned up seven times hotter than usual. But here's how you know that God don't like ugly. The fire was so hot that the flames ended up killing the soldiers who threw the boys in. When Nebuchadnezzar peeked into the furnace, he was shocked to find four unharmed men walking around like nothing had happened instead of three bound boys, and one of the men even looked like Jesus.[2]

In the midst of whatever fires are blazing in your life, God's covering is the best blanket. If He was with Dem Boyz in the furnace, then trust and believe that He's with you right now, in your own heated situation. When Nebuchadnezzar realized that God was protecting the boys, he immediately ordered their release. They stepped outta that furnace like prom night, looking so fresh and so clean. Let that resonate for you in whatever you're facing. Sure, situations will try to burn you emotionally, financially, or professionally, but when it's all said and done, the fire won't consume you, the flames won't singe your clothes; heck, you won't even so much as *smell* like smoke. That's God's way of saying, "When I'm done with you, there won't be any evidence of what you've been through, only evidence of My grace that brought you through."

God's covering is the best blanket.

The book of Isaiah says that God refines and tests us in the furnace of affliction.[3] We're meant to be refined by our fires, not overtaken by them. The flames aren't a punishment; they're a rite of passage. Some challenges are nothing more than litmus tests to see if we'll emerge

2. See Daniel 3:24–25.
3. See Isaiah 48:10.

more damaged or more brilliant than before. A metal goes into fire and comes out as gold. Paper hits flames and turns to ash. Which will you be? Gold, or ash? The truth is, we all have the ability to step out as gold, but too many of us let fear, doubt, and worry burden us to ashes.

The best part about Shadrach & Co.'s story is that when they passed their fiery faith test, the king's response was to elevate them in status and issue an executive order promising to inflict bodily harm on anybody who dared to badmouth their God. Through their resolve, Nebuchadnezzar was turned from a foe to an ally. That's why Jesus loves bamboozling us so much. He knows that when the very thing meant to take us out becomes the very thing that raises us higher, it'll point people back to His glory.

God tricks us into our best lives by using pressure to prune us for purpose. It's His job to trim off every problematic part of us, like a split end. I once heard Bishop Jakes say that, when God gets ready to take you up, He always cuts you back. Remember that the next time your circumstances feel unbearable—it's just God preparing you to skyrocket. Remain joyful in hope, patient in affliction, and faithful in prayer, like Romans teaches us. Resist the urge to quit. Don't stop short of your miracle just because the world applied a little pressure. Push back. Keep rising above the discomfort, and keep believing that this, too, shall pass. Pretty soon you'll be so refined that folks will be blinded by all your shine.

> Some challenges are...litmus tests to see if we'll emerge more damaged or more brilliant than before.

PART II

The Building

CHAPTER 7

MIRACLES DON'T MAKE RESERVATIONS

Although I didn't allow the production company to play me for a fool, losing the opportunity to have my own talk show definitely sent depression knocking at my door. Every passing day became more of a mental, physical, and spiritual struggle. While other people were out enjoying the LA sunshine, I would sit in my apartment, shades closed, in the middle of the day, purposely not letting any light in. Light felt too much like hope, and personally, I'd been let down one too many times by hope. My roommate, Ester, would step into the darkness and remind me that she didn't sign a lease with a vampire, then promptly proceed to open all the curtains.

In an act of defiance, I'd retreat into my bedroom, where it was safe to be sad without judgment, and mourn my dreams deferred. If God could've just sent a playbook so I could run it, that would've made life a thousand times easier. But there was no book; just me feeling like I'd been played for playing by the rules. I was doing everything

I knew to do—performing, volunteering, praying, serving, studying, networking—you name it, I did it. Yet nothing remotely resembling progress was happening in my life. I felt like David in Psalm 73 when he said, "Surely in vain I have kept my heart pure…All day long I've been afflicted, and every morning brings new punishment" (vv. 13–14 NIV).

I had finally reached my breaking point.

It's a lot easier to bounce back when you've been knocked down once. You got stamina and strength to try again. Get knocked down a second time and the rise back up is a little uglier, a lot less graceful. Your legs are wobbly, but you manage to make it on your feet. But that third time, you start to think, *You know what? If I just stay down, life can't throw any more punches at me.*

That's where I was.

It's a pretty weird feeling to be the strong one—the one who makes everyone laugh, the one who brings encouragement in the group chat—only to find yourself in need of a laugh when nothing in the world seems funny. You avoid community because no one's supposed to see you like this. When friends try to cheer you up, you receive it with a smile, but deep down, you despise their positivity because what's the point of getting your hopes up only to be let down again?

While I wallowed in the barrenness of nothing even mattering anyway, I stumbled upon a sermon by Pastor Christine Caine. In it, she said that "Impossible is where God starts and miracles are what God does." I was at impossible and it would take a miracle to get me outta my funk. I tried, once more, to find hope in a morsel of "maybe" still left in me. Like, *Maybe, just maybe, this isn't how my story ends.*

Maybe, a "maybe" is all you've got right now. Heck, maybe the only reason you're reading this book is for me to let you know that your mustard-seed-maybe is enough to see you through. If so, I got'chyu. Every day, I galvanized myself to make moves from a "maybe."

Yvonne, maybe this is temporary. *Brushes teeth.*

Maybe there's still some fight in me left. *Brushes teeth *and* showers.*

Maybe God hasn't forgotten about me, after all. *Brushes teeth, showers, puts on makeup.*

Maybe my blessing is on the other side of my door. *Brushes teeth, showers, puts on makeup, walks outside with expectancy.*

This went on for weeks, and ultimately, moving from a maybe allowed me to hold on to hope against all hope. Until the night of October 22, 2014. That's when my knees buckled on Sunset Boulevard. With hot tears streaming down my face, I yelled, like a madman, into the street, 'cuz I just couldn't take it anymore. I finally gave myself permission to let God know I was pissed at Him for selling me on dreams that felt more like horrible nightmares.

That night was especially triggering because I'd actually worked up the nerve to step out in public and attend the NBC Short Cuts Film Festival. Each year, the festival highlights undiscovered artists who've taken the initiative to create dope work. That work is then screened in front of industry professionals who have the power to further the artist's career. As I watched those young hopefuls excelling at their craft, I was hit with varying emotions. On the one hand, I was genuinely happy for the recognition their art was garnering. On the other hand, I wondered when *I* would produce something of note that could be equally celebrated. I left, feeling both

Find hope in a morsel of "maybe."

inspired and defeated. Holding my composure, I exited the event with a smile, but as soon as my feet hit the hard concrete, the levee holding back my tears broke.

At first they began as a slow, confused trickle, and then escalated into a convulsing, sobbing mess. Unable to control myself, I collapsed. Thankfully, my best friend, Hari, was there to catch my fall. What should've been a three-block walk back home turned into a three-mile gripe fest. *"This doesn't make any sense, Jesus!"* I yelled into the darkness. *"I didn't ask for any of this! I could be a doctor by now. Sure, a miserable one, but a doctor nonetheless, and that would be better than the no-name nobody I currently am. Trying to live out this dream You force-fed me has gotten me nowhere but further into debt."*

I was giving God my best shots and laying out the laundry list of ways He'd fallen short on His promises to me. How dare He do this to *me?* I was one of His foot soldiers—His favorite. It wasn't fair, and I was tired. But real talk, as mad as I was with God, I was even more mad at myself for refusing to throw in the towel. I wanted to give up so bad, but I was already in too deep.

If my meltdown had happened two years before it did, I wouldn't have been nearly as invested. It would've been super easy for me to accept defeat, chuck up the deuces, and call my momma to apologize and ask if I could come home to grab some food. But with four years of skin in the game, I couldn't bring myself to that point—not because of pride, but because somewhere deep in the crevasses of my soul, hanging on by a thread, was the belief that God couldn't be a complete liar. I had sold hope to too many people for me to now turn around and believe that same product was counterfeit.

When I got finished with my entitled, self-righteous rant around mile two, I heard Holy Spirit calmly whisper, *"What's in your hand?"* Well, that got me all fired up again: *"What's in my hand?!"* I yelled back. *"Are You serious right now, Jesus? I got nothing in my hand. If I had anything in it, I wouldn't be crying on Sunset Boulevard. I'm sick of all'a these proverbs and riddles. Just shoot straight with me, Fam. What do you want me to do so I can do it, 'cuz I've done everything else!"*

Crickets.

The whisper was gone and so was my strength. The only logical thing left to do was go to sleep. Right now, if you're feeling exhausted by life, and worn-out from being perpetually disappointed, lemme suggest that, no matter what time it is, and no matter where you are, simply shut this book and go night-night. I believe in the #NapMinistry, and like a Snickers commercial, you're not you when you're tired. Don't worry, I'll wait. This book ain't going nowhere.

> Somewhere deep in the crevasses of my soul, hanging on by a thread, was the belief that God couldn't be a complete liar.

After taking my own advice, I woke up the next morning needing an answer to my anger, so I grabbed Da Good Book. I've had the same DGB since freshman year of college, so roughly twenty years. The pages are all marked up, and some are even falling out. We've been through a lot together and I *know* my Word. So when I opened it that day, searching for anything that would spark even the tiniest bit of peace, I was surprised to land on Psalms 31. Of all the highlights and writings in margins, these verses were left untouched—seemingly insignificant. But there in my room, trying to see a way out of the fog, I read these words that hit like a shot of adrenaline:

"But I trust in you, LORD...My times are in your hands" (vv. 14–15 NIV).

I can't explain it, but for whatever reason, those simple words, *I trust you. My times are in your hands*, became enough. I don't think I'd ever fully understood the term "Bread of Life" as it relates to Jesus or the Word of God, but chewing on that sentence, I suddenly became full and revived, as if revived from a deep coma. I promise you, these are not just fancy words to throw in a book. This was a real feeling in a real moment that really happened. I sat in bed wondering if this was the answer to the question Jesus had posed the night before, *"What's in your hand?" My times* are in Your hands?

I realized the question to me was less about naming tangible items and more of an exercise in finding my Source. God needed me to see beyond the physical emptiness of my actual hands and look instead at the possibilities that existed when I placed my situation at the altar. It was time to release my timelines and surrender all expectations. That was a tall order, but I figured I'd had my dreams in my own hands long enough, and clearly that wasn't working, so I might as well try Jesus. That didn't stop me from getting gangstarr with Him, though. I definitely yelled, *"Yo! You got one more shot, J! If I give it my all this time and it still don't work, then I'm renegotiating the contract!"*

You gotta be some kind of crazy to give Jesus an ultimatum, but that's exactly what I did. I knew that this was my last hoorah, and if it failed, I'd be forced to move back home to Laurel, Maryland, where dreams go to die, and I wasn't tryna go out like that. Not long after my ultimatum, I heard Holy Spirit say, *"I gave you something in your hand that you've done nothing with. Instead, you've busied yourself into believing you've been working hard, when in reality, you've been lazy with what I've purposed you to do."* Deng. He ain't have to say it like that, but He was right. Here I was thinking I was the one doing God all the favors, when really, I was the one short-circuiting my blessing the entire time.

Years earlier, God had given me the concept for my own TV series— *FirstGen*—but I had completely neglected it because I didn't think I was skilled enough to write it. I'd taken a class on TV writing and even attempted a first draft, but eventually, I let it fall by the wayside. My focus shifted to supporting other people's visions because that was easier than taking a chance on my own thing and risking failure. Eventually, I got comfortable with the little bit of money I started making. But, you see, the problem with having money without purpose is that money eventually runs out. Purpose, on the other hand, produces seeds. Those seeds produce trees. And those trees constantly generate fruit.

Fear had rendered me fruitless, and God wanted to resurrect my potential. But in order to raise me up, some things had to die. In her message, Christine Caine stressed that it's only when we come to the end of ourselves that God even shows up. He'll wait until we think our promises have expired and there's no chance for them to happen without divine intervention. That way, when He does what only He can do, only He can take the credit

> I'd had my dreams in my own hands long enough, and clearly that wasn't working, so I might as well try Jesus.

for it. This was my wake-up call, and God wanted my full, undivided attention. Had He not forced me into one of my loneliest and most tragic seasons, I would still be stuck on the treadmill of life, running full speed and getting nowhere fast. For the first time in a long time, I had a clear course of action and I truly believed that God would move Heaven and Hell to help me achieve it.

Much like cocaine, belief is one heck of a drug. When it gets into your system, it compels you to do unorthodox things. Going beast-mode this time wasn't gon'cut it. I had to go full crackhead mode on this one. Now, I ain't condoning, nor have I ever used illicit drugs, but growing up in the DC Metropolitan area at the height of the war on drugs, I've seen my fair share of individuals addicted to crack cocaine. And never not once have I ever heard a crackhead say, "I ain't smoking today 'cuz I ain't got no money." Nope. Not at all. If they want it bad enough, they'll hustle hard for a hit—even if it means peddling micro-waves on a bicycle to make a trade, and if it came to it, throwing in the bike for good measure.

In similar fashion, I was a crazed woman on a mission, and from October 2014 to October 2015, my life literally got flipped, turned upside-down like the Fresh Prince. I detail the events of those glorious twelve months in subsequent chapters, but here's a quick snapshot of what went down.

October 2014: Impossible situation leads to one last shot.

November 2014: Finish *FirstGen* script and host a table read for feedback.

December 2014 to February 2015: Fundraise to shoot *FirstGen* teaser trailer.

February 2015: Shoot trailer.

April 2015: Trailer is released and goes viral.

May 2015: Connect with David Oyelowo to become executive producer.

June 2015: Pitch *FirstGen* to networks.

July 2015: Audition for *Insecure*.

August 2015: Book role of Molly on *Insecure*.

October 2015: Shoot the pilot episode of *Insecure*; able to pay off debts.

In one short year, I went from impossible to *all* things are possible!

All'a that happened only after I put my all into the one who gave His all. So what's still in your hands that needs to be transferred to God's? We tie His hands the minute we think that we can do life on our own terms and in our own ability. Sadly, your own ability can only but take you so far. When we're so full of ourselves and think that, on our own, we're smart enough, capable enough, or connected enough, somewhere down the line we'll actually believe that we had something to do with God's blessings. So He'll let us exhaust ourselves by calling our girlfriends, our homeboys, our favorite aunty, and when everybody comes up short and absolutely no one can help, that's the sweet spot of surrender where God does some of His finest work.

> When everybody comes up short and absolutely no one can help, that's the sweet spot of surrender where God does some of His finest work.

That same spot is where Mary and her sister, Martha, found themselves in Da Good Book. Jesus was their play cousin, so naturally when their brother, Lazarus, got sick, they called on Him to save the day. When Jesus heard the news, He declared, "This sickness will not end in death."[1] Wouldn't it be nice to get verbal assurances from Jesus directly? Can you imagine Him telling you, *"This relationship will be a complete waste of your time. This is the right job for you. This house is a money pit."* Think of how much time and heartache we would save! But then again, think of how much more underdeveloped our faith would be. I know you don't wanna hear this right now, but sometimes, you gotta *go* through some things in order to *grow* through some things.

Mary and Martha definitely weren't tryna hear that because Lazarus *did* die, and it was all Jesus' fault.

PLOT TWIST!

Instead of rushing to meet the sisters when they sent word, Jesus stayed where He was for an extra two days. The whole time they thought they were calling in a lifeline, Jesus was busy yoga posing and nah'mastaying right where He was.

I can only imagine how hopeless it must feel to have direct access to Jesus, the ultimate plug, and it still not be enough to help get you out of your troubles. But God was working on something. You see, miracles don't make reservations. They don't take appointments. They're the epitome of a walk-in. They just show up. When Jesus heard Laz had died, He told His disciples, "For your sake I am glad I was not there, so that you may believe."[2] Not exactly the eulogy you'd expect, but apparently, for *your* sake, there are some things that Jesus will purposely allow

---

1. John 11:4 NIV.
2. John 11:15 NIV.

to (not) happen, so you might believe in greater possibilities. Maybe you're at a point where you don't trust that God can bring you a spouse, so you start manipulating and manufacturing situationships. Sure, it feels good in the moment, but you and God both know that ain't it. So for your sake, God'll start shutting down every Tinder date, every booty call, even every foodie call. And He'll keep shutting them down until there's no opportunity for you to attach your hopes, your joy, or your peace to anything that doesn't have Him at the center. He's selfish like that.

In Mary and Martha's case, they struggled to understand where to place their hope. By the time Jesus arrived, Laz had already been in a morgue for four days. That's a long time to be in a dead situation and still believe God could turn it around. Martha wasted no time in giving Jesus a piece of her mind. As far as she was concerned, Lazarus would've still been alive had Jesus not been working on CP time. Even though they were close, she couldn't see what was in Jesus' hand. She didn't know yet that whatever she needed Him to be, He already was. She needed a revival for her brother; well, Jesus is the resurrection. She needed a miracle; He's the Miracle Maker.

In Exodus 3:14, God says, "I AM THAT I AM" (KJV). It's written without punctuation, but I like to break it up like this: "I am *that*. I am." Essentially, God is saying, fill in the blank. Whatever your "that" is, I'm it, and then He double confirms it. So the passage could read, "I am provision. Really, I am." "I

> Miracles don't make reservations. They don't take appointments. They're the epitome of a walk-in. They just show up.

am confidence. Truly, I am." Still, it's understandable why Martha was apprehensive about getting her hopes up, though. No one had ever seen the miracle Jesus was about to perform. It was virtually impossible to believe for something they didn't even know could exist.

The mourners who'd gathered to pay their respects also weren't helping. They did little to boost the family's confidence in Jesus. In fact, they started badmouthing Him, talkin'bout, "If He could open the blind eyes of a stranger, how come He couldn't keep His friend alive?"[3] Who we surround ourselves with, and the voices we allow to permeate our spirits during challenging times, is extremely crucial. The right folks can inspire hope. The wrong ones can breed dissension.

Jesus wasn't fazed by the critics, tho. If this were the Oscars, He'd win the Academy Award for Best Director, because He orchestrated the whole thing masterfully from beginning to end. There were Mary and Martha crying and pointing fingers, the general public doubting, and a dead man four days in the tomb. Add to that, the pungent, repulsive stench of decay. The stakes were high, but Jesus eats this for breakfast! With the scene set and the cameras rolling, He yelled a proverbial, "ACTION!" in the form of a simple prayer: *Father, I thank you that you have heard me. I knew that you always hear me, but I said this for the benefit of the people standing here, that they may believe.*[4] And with a single command, Lazarus, the man who had been dead *dead*, came walking out of the tomb.

No one else could take the credit for that, and that's the way God likes it.

It's interesting that Jesus endured the tears, the frustration, and the

---

3. See John 11:37.
4. John 11:41–42 NIV.

character assassination simply for the benefit of those standing about. Could it be that when we're not moved by our circumstances, we in turn inspire faith in others? If that's the case, then the opposite is also true. In Proverbs, it says that when we fall to pieces in a crisis, there wasn't much to us in the first place. Deng! That hurt *my* feelings, but they're not wrong. Pastor Mike would always ask, "If you are the only Jesus that some people will ever see, is God in trouble?" Chew on that for a hot second.

God wants to get some credit out of our lives, and He does so through our responses in tough times. Some of your friends, coworkers, classmates, or family members will never step foot into a church, but they will see *you* on full display at the next cookout or holiday party. Will how you handle setbacks be enough of an example to inspire them to believe?

No pressure, but pressure.

We already saw how the sisters dealt with the aftermath of a dead situation, but what about Lazarus? He actually endured the dead situation. It was *him* who took his last breath. *Him* whose heart stopped beating. *Him* whose life ended. In your case, you're the one whose business folded. You lost the house, the scholarship, the chance to go pro. You're the one living in the thick of your impossible situation, and like Lazarus, sometimes God needs you to be the sacrificial lamb in your own story. But don't trip, tho. That's not where your story ends. If He did it before, He can do it again, so you can count on being raised up.

When all the chips are down and you can't get through the miracle reservation

> Sometimes God needs you to be the sacrificial lamb in your own story.

hotline, let these words that Holy Spirit spoke over me, shortly after my own breakdown, resuscitate your dry bones and restore your dead dreams:

"I have not forgotten you. I will accomplish everything I placed in your heart. The world works by man's schedule, but I created man. My timing is perfect. I alone am God. I need nothing added and nothing can be removed. Just wait, have faith and watch…See and be amazed…I can do more in a matter of weeks than you have experienced all year. It is not over yet. Get back up. Get back in and win. Win!…Get excited again. There is enough time. Because I am more than enough."

CHAPTER 8

IF YOU STAY READY, YOU AIN'T GOTTA GET READY

If you've never heard the term "Linsanity," pause now to Google it. Hopefully you fell down a steep rabbit hole over the 2012 New York Knicks phenom, Jeremy Lin. A relative unknown, Lin was stuck in the D-League until desperation, injuries, and a series of other (un)fortunate events thrust him into the Knicks starting lineup. The kid who had only played a total of 55 minutes in 23 games that season went on to revitalize the franchise in an astonishing seven-game winning streak and became an international sensation.

While most people will only ever search for the highlight reel, it's important to know that getting bamboozled by Jesus often includes a journey of lows and highs. In Jeremy's case, there was a perfect storm of luck, grace, and chaos that had to exist in order for Linsanity to be Googleable. First there had to be an NBA lockout, delaying the season and adding pressure to players and coaches alike. Then the team in need of a miracle had to be located in a major market, like New York, and the source of said miracle had to be an unlikely Asian-American athlete.

Adding to the mayhem, the Knicks had to spend a premium to acquire Carmelo Anthony, leaving them with no funds to afford a prominent point guard. Lin then had to be cut by two separate teams, freeing him up to be signed by the Knicks as one of their four backup points. But then Lin also had to get demoted to the D-League, leaving him to wonder about his future while crashing on his teammate's couch. Then the Knicks had to lose ten games straight, and the three point guards ahead of Lin on the Knicks roster all had to get benched or injured. With nothing *more* to lose, the Knicks' head coach, Mike D'Antoni, had to get desperate enough to call Lin up from the D-league and throw him in a game for the heck of it. While all eyes were on him, Lin had to come from relative obscurity to score 25 points to give the Knicks their first of seven straight wins, which included a klutch victory over Kobe Bryant's Lakers.

Many people would start the story of Jeremy's amazing run at that last sentence. But the reality is, the run never happens without all the preparation Jeremy put in behind the scenes. In the off-season, coaches say that he was the first to arrive at practice and the last to leave. He would study game tape, improve his jump shot, and increase his quickness on the court. Basically, Lin stayed ready so he didn't have to *get* ready when Coach D'Antoni put him in that fateful game.

Preparing for your big moment like it could come at *any* moment, is what staying ready so you don't have to get ready means. Your day *is* coming, your opportunity *will* arise, but the question is, will *you* rise to the occasion? Lissen, I know it's scary to be the first one in your family to forge a path without any blueprints. It's an isolating and pretty risky process. How do you know if you're making the right moves? *You don't.* Will any of this actually work? *Maybe. Maybe not.* The stakes are dangerously high and the outcome, highly uncertain.

When my parents strongly opposed my career switch from medical doctor to "jester," as my mom called it, I wished I could've calmed their fears and assured them that things would work, but I didn't know that for certain. I *hoped* they would. I *believed* it was possible. But the same way Jeremy Lin didn't know that one day he'd be in the D-League and the very next week he'd be selling out stadiums, there was no way I could've predicted when my big break would come. All I could do was prepare for that moment, like I expected it to happen.

> *Your day is coming, your opportunity will arise, but the question is, will you rise to the occasion?*

I had a choice to make: Do I upset the parents who'd sacrificed greatly for me, or do I risk not following through on what I was called to do? It wasn't easy, but ultimately, I decided that I loved God more than I hated disappointing my parents. Along the way, God provided bite-sized blessings to get me to my next step, where more bites awaited. That's the protocol for getting bamboozled: You trust, you do, you wait, you repeat, until the moment that changes your life happens.

While living in New York, a fellow artist told me he was traveling to LA to meet with casting directors, in hopes of stacking up auditions. I could feel the rumblings of jealousy rising in me. *"I want to go to LA, too!"* I sulked to God later that night. As soon as the words left my mouth, I heard Him reply, *"Well, what does it take to get to LA?"* With hesitation, I answered, *"A plane ticket?"* and God shot back, *"Exactly. So you don't need to be jealous, you just need to pick a date and a seat number."*

I ain't like His tone, but He wasn't wrong. So often we neglect the practical, tangible steps we can take because we're busy "waiting on a sign from the Lord," when half the time, God is waiting on *us* to make a move. That's spiritual procrastination, which ain't nothing but the devil wrapped up in Häagen-Dazs ice cream. It sounds good, but it'll get'chyu got. Instead, we gotta get like the rapper Ludacris and adopt a "When I move, You move—just like that!" mindset with Jesus. If you're thinking, *Hol'up. That ain't right. Don't Da Good Book say, "Many are the plans in a person's heart, but it is the LORD's purpose that prevails"?* [1] Yeah, it does say that, but at some point, we're gonna have to formulate a plan and actually *give* Jesus something to prevail over.

I'm aware that common sense is no longer common, but we gon'have to bring that suckka back like pumpkin spice in the fall. Don't get me wrong, I'm not telling you to go be reckless and leave Jesus outta the equation. That ain't it. But, you can certainly generate your own ideas and check to see if He rocks with them or nah. If He does, then you've got your marching orders. If He doesn't, you *still* have your marching orders: Head back to the drawing board and think of another idea to run past Him. In every scenario, you're actively participating in the events of your life and staying ready for whatever might come next.

After God told me to pick a date, I looked at my calendar and realized it was about to be peak wedding season. Since emceeing events was how I made my living at that time, taking myself out the mix would

---

1. Proverbs 19:21 NIV.

put a serious strain on my finances. But the only way to break the mold was to actually break outta the mold. I already knew the level wedding hosting would take me; now it was time to discover how far I could reach in LA.

There comes a point in your life when you have to sacrifice the familiar to take hold of the fantastic. The familiar waits for life to happen, but the fantastic grabs it by the horns—and I was holding on with both hands. I blocked out what I thought were random dates, and didn't book any weddings for the six weeks I planned to be gone. I reached out to the only two people I knew in LA, Kenny and ChiChi—the couple who ran the pageant that started me on my comedic journey—but they were busy with their newborn baby.

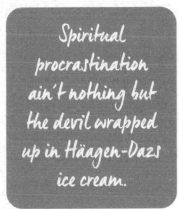

As fate would have it, one day, as I was scrolling through Facebook, I landed on the page of a guy named Michael Ajakwe. His last name was a dead giveaway that he was part of the Igbo tribe, like I was. When I read his bio, I did a double-take when he mentioned skipping med school to pursue a career in TV writing. Was this guy the male version of *me*? Without thinking twice, I sent him a private message telling him all about our similarities, and how I would be coming to LA to find work, and I asked if he had the hookup.

Now let's pause for a second: If I hadn't used wisdom to apply practical steps, then I wouldn't have had actual dates available to give to Mike, and without that, I would've just seemed like another unserious actress, just hoping-and-a-wishing for someone to give her a chance. I get messages all the time from people saying that they would gladly move to New York or LA if they already had a job waiting for them in either city. That's a very safe, logical, and fiscally responsible plan, and I'm sure it may work for some—but safe, logical, and fiscally responsible are just...*that*. You know exactly what to expect from them.

The people who live in those confinements never shift culture. They're never part of the larger conversation, and honestly, they don't get a lot of shine. Now, I'm not in your pockets counting your coins, so don't go moving to LA and become homeless, talkin'bout, "Well, Yvonne told me to stay ready!" No, ma'am. No, sir. That. ain't. it. *At all.* What I'm saying is don't be afraid to shake up safe. Do something radical that gets God's attention. You know what doesn't get His attention? All your excuses. They get His frustration—I know, 'cuz they frustrate the heck outta me too.

But God, does that mean I have to leave all my friends behind and start from scratch? You know how hard it is for me to meet new people?

"Buy the ticket."

But God, what if I don't succeed? Then I'll look like a loser whose "faith" doesn't work.

"Follow My lead."

But God, where will I stay? Where will I work? How will I survive?

"Just stay ready."

If God's in it, His response will repeatedly be for you to go for it, 'cuz He's already on the other side awaiting your arrival. I had no clue how things would turn out when I headed to LA. I just knew that I'd spent $350 on a nonrefundable flight and had $900 left to my name to figure something out. Mike eventually responded to my message and asked me to send him footage of my stand-up. Because I stay ready, I mailed him a DVD of a recent show I'd done. A few weeks later, Mike hit me back to let me know that his brother had just gotten married, and family from Lagos to London had flown into town. To entertain them, he'd played my DVD, and that's when he said these magical words: *"Yvonne, you made my mom laugh. I've never seen her laugh so hard, and I'm a comedy writer. I don't know what that says about me or my career, but I know it says that you've got something special, so I'm gonna help you out."*

I was floored. It was like God had orchestrated time, space, preparation, and opportunity to collide in perfect harmony, and there I was ready to take full advantage of it all. When your number gets called up, it's too late to be scrambling to put on your jersey or fumbling to tie your laces. You dun' missed it, and they dun' moved on.

Mike and I chatted for over an hour that day, swapping childhood stories and bonding over our shared experience of being the Black sheep in a Nigerian family (his brother was a doctor, *of course*). He asked me what I wanted to do in LA, and I kept myself open, telling him that I was willing to be the best shoe-shiner or coffee-getter to anyone willing to take a chance on training me. I said this knowing full well that I had a whole entire master's degree, but sometimes the best way up is down. (see chapter 13.)

A couple days later, Mike told me that he'd sent my résumé to the producers of *Love That Girl,* the show he was currently writing on, and they

> Don't be afraid to shake up safe. Do something radical that gets God's attention.

were interested in meeting with me. Y'all, I was so madd hyped and also extremely overwhelmed by Mike's generosity. I had never met this man—not even through FaceTime—and here he was investing so much into me. Even though he stressed that the position would be an *unpaid* internship in the writer's room, I didn't care. Just being able to get my foot in the door would pay off eventually.

The next day, I got a call from Stacey Evans Morgan, an EP on the show. She schooled me on the culture of the room and let me know what my duties would be. Midway through our conversation, Stacey asked if she knew me from somewhere, and I responded, *"It depends— are you a bill collector on the weekends?"* She laughed but persisted that my last name sounded familiar. After throwing out a few possible connections and drawing blanks, we figured it would come to us eventually.

Here's where things got really interesting. We talked on a Friday. The writer's room would be starting the following Monday. Guess what date Monday was? August 2. And guess what date I had randomly booked my flight to land in LA? You guessed it. I can't e'en make this up. That wasn't a random coincidence. That was me staying ready to take advantage of whatever opportunities came my way. At this point, I had a ticket, a job, but still nowhere to live, and only two days left to figure it out.

That Saturday, my parents and I were meant to drive to Ohio for a wedding, but they decided to cancel the trip. Still, I felt the need to attend, so I made the journey to Cleveland by myself. At the wedding, I ran into ChiChi and Kenneth—the only couple I knew in LA—and told them my good news. When I mentioned the name of the studio where I'd be working, ChiChi screamed and said that it was literally down the street from their house. She offered me a spot on their couch, since the nursery had taken up their extra room. She also gave me full access to her car because she was still on maternity leave, and it was just sitting idle.

Do you see what happened there? In June, I got jealous and started putting a plan in place, and in a matter of one weekend, I got a job, housing, and a car to drive. It *all* matters. God uses every single person and every single situation to get you to your designated end, but you have to be ready when He pulls the trigger. I've been told that in the game of football, the quarterback doesn't always throw to a receiver but to a specific spot on the field. It's up to the receiver to dodge defenders and get in position, at just the right time, to make the catch. The problem is, God's been throwing to the spot, we just haven't been in position. Fear and logic have tackled us to the ground and kept us from hitting our mark. It's easy to get mad when our favorite team misses the touchdown pass and loses the game, but when are you gonna start getting heated over the missed goals in your own life?

After starting the internship, it didn't take long for Stacey to figure out where she knew me from. She'd been a producer on a comedy show I shot a few years back that never saw the light of day. However, as producer, she got to watch all the footage and that's how she became familiar with my humor. As a result, she vouched for me in the room. Normally, interns were meant to be seen and never heard, but her stamp of approval gave me the freedom to pitch jokes with other senior-level writers. Eventually, the show's creator, Bentley Kyle Evans,

> When are you gonna start getting heated over the missed goals in your own life?

pulled me aside and asked if I had any other interests. I shared that I wanted to act, and before I knew it, I was auditioning for a small role, which I later booked.

By the end of my trip, the $900 I'd brought with me had faded fast, but I reasoned that at least I'd gained an invaluable experience.

Ohhh, but it gets better.

Always one to outdo Himself, God doesn't just wanna stop at an experience. That's too easy. He didn't just give Jeremy Lin a win or two. He created a spectacle that turned him into a household name. Similarly, He wanted to show me that He could rain down abundance when I least expected it. One day, on set, I was handed an envelope with a check inside for $950…with my name on it. I didn't realize that the role I'd booked came with a payday. I was just happy to be on TV. Here I was thinking I'd lost money, but God replenished it with interest.

After the internship, Mike stayed in my life as a friend and forever advocate. He would bring me in on other projects he worked on and treat me to dinner, as we caught up on life and the latest industry news. One of my last memories of him was in 2018 when I visited him in his hospital room as he battled cancer. By then, I had found success on *Insecure*, and with what frail strength he had left, Mike turned to his mom, sister, and wife, who were all in the room, and proudly boasted, *"She's a big star now, but I gave her her first shot in LA. I always knew she was going to make it."*

You haven't yet met the people or been to the places or done the things that God will use to facilitate the plans He has for you. Don't worry about the whens or the wheres or the hows. All you can be is ready for action when it's go-time. In Da Good Book, Noah exemplified that, even if it got him ridiculed and ostracized.

God had given Noah the task of building an ark because He was gonna make it rain, and not with hunned dolla billz. He instructed Noah to put his family and two of every animal in the boat. Some philosophers believe that, at the time, neither Noah nor any of his neighbors had ever seen or heard of rain. If that's true, talk about walking by faith and not by sight. I can only imagine the confusion Noah caused in his gated community. Picture him hammering away at the side of the ark when his friends came over:

"Hey, Noah! What'chyu doing?"

"Oh, just building the ark before it rains."

"Rain? What's that?"

"Don't know exactly, but God said it was gon'rain water from the sky."

"Water from the…what'chyu talkin'bout, Noah? You telling me the clouds are gonna cry?"

"No clue. Just doing what God told me."

If you were a member of his family, life would've been pretty rough for you as well. Imagine how humiliated his wife, Marge (she feels like a Marge to me), felt as she got a mani-pedi!

"Say, Marge, what kind of boots does one wear…*in the rain?*" inquired the ladies as they snickered.

I wouldn't be surprised if she got home and tried to reason with Noah.

"…So you're *poooositive* it was God? And He for sure said 'rain'?"

"For the hundredth time, babe, yes!"

> You haven't yet met the people or been to the places or done the things that God will use to facilitate the plans He has for you.

"First of all, don't get loud with me. I'm just tryna make sure I understand, 'cuz those heauxz fit'na catch these hands if they keep laughing at me."

Marge is from Baltimore. Don't let the Old Testament name fool you.

You gotta admit, tho, that the situation would sound pretty ridiculous to everyone *but* Noah. In your case, the people around you can't figure out why you're deviating from the norm. They're not convinced that this is the right move for you. They mean well, but you can't let their reservations become your hesitation. Recently, I saw an Instagram post that said, "No one else is supposed to understand your calling, it wasn't a conference call." Now, that'll preach! Nobody was checking for Jeremy Lin to send shockwaves through the world until he did. If he'd allowed his history of getting cut, traded, and demoted to dictate his potential, then there would be no cover spreads, no new lexicon added to our vocabulary, and certainly no documentary made. Similarly, despite all the ridicule, Da Good Book says that Noah "in holy fear built an ark to save his family."[2]

That holy fear is key, and I know all about it. In holy fear, I had to believe the opposite was true when my parents worried that my career would bring shame on the family and hinder my chances of finding a suitable husband. People may laugh at you and call you crazy, but that's because you are. It takes crazy, stupid faith to do what you're doing. Pioneering is hard. So no, you're not supposed to be understood while you're breaking

> People may laugh at you and call you crazy, but that's because you are.

2. Hebrews 11:7 NIV.

barriers. Folks aren't gonna "get" you while you're expanding your world, but expand anyway. Stay focused on becoming your best self even when no one else is watching, because someone is *always* watching. Run the drills, read the trades, study the greats, book the flight, audit the class, write the proposal—do whatever it takes to stay ready. And one sweet day, when your supply is summoned, you'll go from being called insane to making the world *go* insane.

CHAPTER 9

LET GOD, *GOD*

There've been a few occasions when I thought Jesus was crazy. Like, this-don't-make-no-kinda-sense crazy. Like the time He told me to put my half of rent into the offering at church. *"Oh, You dun' lost Your God-given mind, Jesus."* What kind of test was this, and how many more would I need to pass? This class sucks and I want to write a review. While the praise team sang "Oceans," I felt like I was drowning in one. Immediately I started crying because I knew two things to be true: (1) I absolutely did not want to do it and was pissed that God would even ask me to, and (2) I knew I was gonna have to do it anyway. @!#$%*!

Knowing I was gon'do it didn't stop me from arguing and trying to reason my way out of it. *"But, Jesus, You not listening, This doesn't just affect me. What will my roommate do if we're kicked out?"* At the time, Ester and I were the only Black tenants in our West Hollywood apartment building. How would that look if all of our stuff was tossed out on the sidewalk for all to see? C'mon, fam, we can't go out like that!

I tried to explain to Jesus things He already knew, like how I was already short on my half of rent and was tripping over how to make up the difference, and now He was asking for everything I had. Rather than being understanding and considerate, He used my words against me. *"Okay, so if it's not enough anyway, why don't you just trust Me with the little you do have? If you keep it, you'll still be short, but if you give it, there's no telling what I can do."* No, Jesus, TELL. ME. I need to be told everything You can do!

I sat there weighing my options, much like I'm sure the widow woman in 1 Kings did when the prophet Elijah also asked for more than she was willing to give. As the story goes, the widow was extremely poor and had reached the end of her rope. She'd made plans to have one last meal before calling it quits. Well, God didn't like those plans very much, so He threw her a lifeline. Only problem is, God's lifelines don't often look like anything we want to grab hold of. One day, He sent the prophet Elijah to meet the widow, and Elijah asked if she would do him a solid and grab him a glass of water.

No biggie. Water was probably flowing from a well somewhere, so even though it might've been inconvenient, it wasn't unreasonable. Inconvenient, but not unreasonable is how Jesus reels you into getting bamboozled, and perfectly describes how I felt about giving to the church, especially in those days when I didn't have much. I understood the benefits of tithing, or giving 10 percent of your total earnings, so even though that extra bit of money could've gone a long way toward paying bills, I gave it anyway.

> God's lifelines don't often look like anything we want to grab hold of.

Now, I ain't going back and forth with you about whether or not you agree with the practice, 'cuz that's none'a my business. I just know what's worked for me. I do often joke with my business reps, tho, about how unfair it is that I gotta pay them a 10 percent commission. How they gon'get the same amount as Jesus? He died for my sins, and all they did was get me an audition. Well, if they can get a cut, it's only right that I break Jesus off too.

But here's where Jesus plays too much. As the widow was getting the water for Elijah, he had the audacity to ask her for some bread too. With the last bit of strength she had, the woman told Elijah, "No disrespect, sir, but I ain't got it for you. All I got is a lil' bit of flour and some oil back at the crib, and real talk, I was heading that way to go make a loaf so me and my son can eat it and die."[1] What a heartbreaking moment of transparency and vulnerability. She was admitting to herself and this stranger that she'd given up on life and didn't want to keep failing as a person and as a mom. Her problems seemed insurmountable, and now this man was piling on to them. How many of us can relate to this widow's frustration? We've been at that point when all we're trying to do is hold on to our next breath to keep from breaking down, and then all of a sudden, God throws us for a loop.

Elijah heard the woman's protests, but he wasn't moved by them. He stood firm in his request that she first take care of his needs, and promised that if she did, she'd never be broke another day in her life. Reluctantly, the widow took him up on that offer, and just as the prophet said, she and her son lived without ever having to worry about their next meal. I wish I could've gotten that same level of assurance; instead, all Jesus said was, *"It's not enough anyway, so trust Me."*

I was trembling but trusting. Only my version of trust looked like me putting all the cash I had in the offering, and instantly looking

---

1. See 1 Kings 17:12.

around to see who'd been assigned by Heaven to cut me a check. Isn't that how obedience works? I did what God said, I passed the test, now it was His turn to come through emeedjetlee. That's what He did for this widow and also for Abraham.

When Isaac, the son God gave Abraham and Sarah in their old age, grew up, God told Abraham to take him on a little father-son road trip and offer him up as a sacrifice—and by sacrifice, I mean kill him. Scripture doesn't detail if there was an argument between God and Abraham. It just says that God made the request and the next day Abraham was packing up the minivan. Dassit. I wonder if that conversation doesn't exist because Abraham reasoned that the God asking him to sacrifice Isaac was the same God who opened up Sarah's ninety-year-old womb to have the baby in the first place. If God did the impossible before, then he might as well go ahead and let God, *God* it up again.

Anything we can think, dream, ask for, or imagine, God is God enough to do exceedingly, abundantly above that. Abe went as far as building an altar, tying Isaac up, placing him on said altar, and actually raising his knife, before God finally stopped him and provided a ram in the bush to sacrifice instead. That's some next-level display of trust on Abraham's part, but if you're Isaac, you're definitely signing up for therapy to unpack all'a this trauma. Father's Day cards to Abe after this would'a been real coded: *Dear Dad, I'm glad I'm still alive to celebrate you. Love, your first (and almost last) son, Isaac.*

Back in LA, I was dealing with my

> Anything we can think, dream, ask for, or imagine, God is God enough to do exceedingly, abundantly above that.

own traumatic moment. Exactly what I expected to happen, happened. My rent check bounced like big booties in a strip club. I'd given God a whole entire week to supernaturally transfer funds into my account and this was how He repaid me? He could create the earth in six days, but somehow, getting me rent in seven was too much like work? I was certain I'd get evicted, and that's the part that stung the most. My apartment was my most prized possession. Before getting into it, I'd moved three times in four months and felt extremely unstable. The thought of losing it was unbearable.

Pastor Mike would often ask, Do God's blessings have you or do you have them? If they've got you, then more than likely, you're unwilling to surrender them, like I was. If you have *them*, then like Abraham, you can sacrifice them at will. My reaction to the rent debacle revealed that I still treated God like a genie in a bottle. I was basically saying, "I'll give, but hurry up and give it back before I get an overdraft fee." I couldn't see it at the time, but I was more afraid of what my landlord could do than I was resolved to let God, *God* up the situation. That's why He let the check bounce. He needed me to know that I couldn't always dictate *how* He'd show up, but I'd best be certain that He *would* show up.

Once I got the memo, that's when Grace came in the picture.

I got a message from her, telling me that she'd suddenly gotten a writing gig and needed to move from New York to LA that weekend, and was wondering if I knew of a place she could rent from February to May? The timing couldn't have been more perfect. May was when we were slated to start shooting the first season of *Insecure*, and by then I would have steady income. Without much hesitation, I offered her my room to sublet, and her exact reply was, *"I feel like this is divinely inspired because I was so worried about staying with some random stranger. God is Good!"*

I slept on the living room couch while Grace took the bedroom. While it's easy to think of that as a step backward, I looked at it as one of those unorthodox lifelines. God had provided a ram in the bush and was showing me that He could send His grace to meet a need... *literally*. Our living arrangement led to some serious Black girl magic. By the end of that year, Grace's show got nominated for an Emmy, Ester booked her first staff writing gig, and Molly Carter was born— and I've never bounced a check since. The three of us have remained friends, and as luck, fate, or bamboozlement would have it, Grace eventually became a writer on Season 4 of *Insecure*, which also earned me my first Emmy nomination.

God never wastes a lesson. You might not like the class, but be sure to pass the tests. When you let God, *God*, and fully surrender your frustration to His holy imagination, there's no telling what answers He can provide. Even when you think you got your cards lined up, you still can't play Spades with God. He'll always have the Big Joker, ready to trump whatever moves you think are right. He's in your tomorrow today, so if He asks you to do something unprecedented and kinda sorta ridiculous, just rock with it.

> *Surrender your frustration to His holy imagination.*

CHAPTER 10

I SWEAR TO GOD

For my twenty-first birthday, all I wanted was for my mom to make dinner for me and my friends and deliver it to campus. My wish list included her signature jollof rice, plantains, and jerk chicken. I personally didn't think it was too much to ask for. And even if it was, it was a milestone birthday. If ever there was a year to be demanding, that was it. My mom promised to make me whatever I wanted on the weekend, but that wasn't good enough. I insisted on the meal being ready that Thursday, on my actual birthday. Even my friends tried to get me to chill, but I wasn't tryna hear that.

Being the amazing woman that she is, my mom delivered on her promise and came through with a spread of deliciousness. I couldn't have been happier. Or so I thought. Apparently, the reason why everyone was making such a big deal out of my simple request was because my mom was actually planning a huge surprise party for me that weekend—complete with extended family flying in. The friends I'd insisted that my mom cook for were the same ones she'd been conspiring with all along. What I thought was "no big deal" was actually quite burden-some since she had to cook a full meal twice, while working overtime, all so she wouldn't blow the surprise (*woops*).

Unlike my mom with my birthday plans, people make promises all the time that they don't intend on keeping. But when God promises to bless you, He doesn't do so haphazardly. He backs it up with everything that He is. We swear on things that are greater than ourselves, like our mother's grave. But what's greater than God? The only collateral suf-ficient for Him to swear by, is Himself.

Basically, God swears to God He'll bless you.

I'm sure you were raised not to swear to God, and you shouldn't 'cuz you don't have the cachet to back it up. But God does. And when He swears to Himself on your behalf, that settles it. Da Good Book says that God anointed us, set His seal of ownership on us, and put His Spirit in our hearts as a deposit, guaranteeing what is to come.[1] Basically, God's put a down payment on our futures and has given us the title deed to the Kingdom. What's His has become ours, and what's ours is a life littered with surprises of things we didn't know to ask for or even want, until they appeared.

I learned this firsthand, back in 2014, when I was finalizing the script for my show, *FirstGen*—a sitcom about a Nigerian-American family. I knew the idea would be a hard sell to networks, 'cuz this was before the Wakanda era, where movies like *Black Panther* and shows like *Bob Hearts Abishola*

Basically, God's put a down payment on our futures and has given us the title deed to the Kingdom.

---

1. See 2 Corinthians 1:21–22.

normalized depictions of Africa. To visually explain the world I was creating, I decided to shoot a concept trailer.

Problem was, concept trailers cost money and need production teams, neither of which I had. But God swore to God back on Sunset Boulevard to bless me and keep me from moving back to Laurel, Maryland. So it didn't surprise me when, during a casual meeting with a few women from church, I asked if anyone had connections to an independent production company, and one of the ladies said that her boyfriend's cousin, Elaine, managed one.

Of course she did.

When there's a blessing with your name on it, God'll assign the right people to be compelled to help you. Elaine was the right people. She agreed to waive her fee and take on the project at a rate discounted from $10k to $7k. That rate was predicated on me finding a location to film for free. In *LA*? (Jesus be a real estate agent.) On top of that, I had four short weeks to come up with the funds. While I appreciated the hookup, $7k was still above my budget. In fact, zero thousand dollars was above the budget, but God swore to God.

To raise money, I opted out of doing a Kickstarter or GoFundMe campaign and took the more personal approach of petitioning family and friends for donations. It was slow going for a while, but I kept believing that God wouldn't fill me up to leave me on E. Friends suggested that maybe I should pump the brakes, and not get so hung up on the project. That was easy for them to say from behind the desks of their comfortable day jobs. But I couldn't let up. I watched the trailer for every comedy that premiered on ABC that year to ensure that mine had the same quality. I attended plays to collect headshots of potential actors, hosted street-style interviews about African trivia with tourists on Hollywood Boulevard, and with the help of friends, even created a mini documentary to highlight stories from other immigrant groups. But I was still short on funds.

Then one day, my neighbor Melissa saw me hustling to create more content for the show. To lend her support, she asked, "Would it help if I gave you $1,500?" Umm…Melissa, it would *always* help to get $1,500. (Also, where were you when I needed rent money?) She confessed that it was refreshing to see me working so hard, tryna make things shake, because it reminded her of the grind she'd had when she first moved to the city. The tears that flowed from my eyes were hot and real. The fact that my faith in action caused someone to put money behind my dream, when they didn't have to, was beyond overwhelming.

Her seed money put us at the $2,250 mark, and I fasted, prayed, and hustled for weeks in anticipation of God meeting our goal. A day before the initial $5,000 deposit was due, I still only had $3,225 toward the project. It was looking like I was gonna have to push production. Around 3 a.m. while I was doing edits for a promo video, I got a message from my friend Julius in Nigeria, asking me what *FirstGen* was all about. I was tired and tempted to not engage, but instantly, I heard Holy Spirit say, *"Don't hold back,"* so I indulged his many questions. He asked about my ideal network for the show, how I would pivot if it didn't sell, if I would consider turning it into a web series, and on and on. At one point, I thought, *Am I being audited, because, bruhh!* but I patiently answered him and finally, after the interrogation, he said that I could "count on him for three."

God wouldn't fill me up to leave me on E.

I remember thinking, *Fam, you kept me up for just three hundred dollars?!* You ever been grateful and disappointed at the same time? That was me. But the next day, I woke up to an alert that three *thousand* dollars had been transferred into the account! I'd made the deadline and officially had enough money to shoot! When God swears to God to bless you, He'll tilt Heaven toward Earth, transcend time zones, and pierce the hearts of men to get you to the finish line. You better believe there's a blessing with your name on it when money gets wired from Nigeria to America—and it's not an email scam from a prince with an inheritance! (I'm just joking; that only happens in Ghana.)

> When God swears to God to bless you, He'll tilt Heaven toward Earth, transcend time zones, and pierce the hearts of men to get you to the finish line.

Even though I finally had the funds, I still needed a house to film in. But God wasn't done God-ing up the situation. Later that day, I attended a friend's baby shower, and as soon as I walked into the home, all I saw was opportunity. It was an oversized duplex, so it was spacious enough to pass camera equipment through. I offered the owner cleaning services and a day trip to the beach in exchange for the location, and she graciously accepted. In a single day, I'd met my budget and secured a venue. You can't tell me God ain't real!

What need of yours is God swearing to God on your behalf for today? Is He saying, I swear to God your marriage isn't over? I swear to God this sickness won't take you out? I swear to God you haven't missed your moment? With all the backing of Heaven, you can rest assured that if God swore it, He'll go to war for it. And war is exactly what He thrust a guy named Gideon into in Da Good Book.

Gideon was living a rather mediocre existence, until, one day, an angel appeared, calling him a mighty warrior. Clearly, Gideon thought there was a mix-up. As far as he was concerned, his clan was at the bottom of the totem pole and he himself was the weakest link. What he didn't realize was that God had chosen him to save the Israelites from the Midianite army.

Unconvinced, Gideon threw out several reasons why he wasn't the right man for the job. He was steady tryna block his own blessings, like I was with my birthday party, but God wasn't having it. In his sermon "I Didn't Know I Was Me," Bishop Jakes shared that we convey to others not to expect too much from us through our inaccurate depictions of ourselves. The excuses we make support who we think we are and offer us a license to blame someone else for what we didn't become.

God is not interested in you staying small. Why show up to accept second place when first already has your name on it? After God swears to Himself on your behalf, you should be unsettled by settling. Recently, I saw an IG post that made me chuckle, but also gave me pause. It said, "Don't ever settle. Not for a job, a man, an acrylic set not shaped correctly, nothing." God swore to God for you to *be* too picky and to have everything He set out for you to have. He's not willing to allow the good deposit He placed inside of you to

> *If God swore it, He'll go to war for it.*

go to waste. Hear me clearly: You are more than what you believe you're capable of. You've been called out of your old self, out of your former expectations, and out of your own self-imposed limitations, into the more that's available and waiting for you to tap into.

Gideon was still hesitant about going into battle, so God sent him into enemy territory to eavesdrop on a conversation where a man was describing a dream that had him shook. In the dream, the entire Midianite camp had been struck down by Gideon's sword. Check how strategic God is. He predisposed Gideon's enemies to fear him before he even waged a war. The same guy who, a few paragraphs ago, was convinced he was worthless was now the one who had his opponents scared to death. Whether you realize there's a blessing with your name on it or not doesn't stop it from existing. Other people see it, even if you don't. And if you refuse to act on it, you'll forfeit it, while they take advantage of it.

When you think about that big, scary opportunity that has you feeling as inept as Gideon, you might be tempted to ask, "Why me?" but instead, ask yourself, "Why *not* me?" Why *not* you, who's been praying and preparing for this moment? You, who's been purposed for such a time as this? Asking "Why me?" is actually an insult to God. It insinuates that somehow He made a mistake by hand-selecting you to live out those goals. It begs for validation to make you feel good about yourself, and low-key, it wants to point to personal effort as justification for the blessings when they come. But you can't take God's credit, and to make sure of it, He'll throw audibles in your plans, like He did to Gideon.

Right when Gideon worked up enough nerve to fight, God told him to trim his army from thirty-two thousand soldiers to a raggedy three hundred. He also instructed the men *not* to attack. They weren't to lift a single finger, but rather were commanded to lift their trumpets instead. The battle would be won, not with heavy artillery, but with weapons of worship. When all three hundred trumpets blared in unison, God caused the sound to create so much confusion within the enemy's camp that the Midianites ended up killing each other. There are some battles God will send you into, but because He's already sworn to Himself to bless you, you won't even have to break a sweat.

While Gideon was praying for a way out, God was intentionally sending him in. He'd been asking God to provide the very thing that was already in his DNA. Your answer is in you. In fact, your answer *is* you. You are who you've been waiting on to release your own blessing. I was praying for God to send a job offer, a TV role, an agent or manager, but instead, God sent me to battle for my breakthrough.

Winning is in the cards for you. God sealed it with Jesus. He guaranteed it with the Blood. And He's signed your name on the dotted line. He's saying to you today, "I swear to God I'm gon' bless you." Just like He did with Gideon, He's sending angels to call you into your true identity. You were made for this moment. You're equipped for this challenge. Don't let you be the last one to know you're *you*.

> *Your answer is in you. In fact, your answer is you.*

CHAPTER 11

FEAR IS FOOD POISONING, BUT REGRET IS HERPES

I n our house in Maryland, we had this multicolored sectional couch in the family room. It was spacious and comfortable, but there was one spot in particular that was coveted by me and my brothers. It was the part where you could really stretch out your legs fully, and the best thing about it was that it went to whoever got there first. Given where I fell in the birth pecking order, that was a rare advantage. All I had to do was call first dibs.

The problem was, because I was the youngest, even if I did get to the couch first, I didn't have the luxury of leaving that spot for any reason. If I did, my brothers would muscle their way in, and I'd lose the lay-out for good. So I held my appetite, my pee, and anything else that threatened my position. We had a rule that you couldn't fall asleep on the couch, or you'd be sent to your room. Well, one night, I'd gained control of the infamous spot, but I hadn't gained control of my eyelids. As I fought sleep with overextended blinks, I could hear the warnings. *"Yvonne, if you're sleepy, go upstairs."*

Defiantly, I stayed, even though I was fading fast. *"Leave me alone, I'm awake,"* I lied. I can't tell you what happened next. All I know is that halfway through the night, I woke up to find myself lying on the carpet *outside* my bedroom door. Because I'd fallen asleep on the couch, one of my brothers had gone through the trouble of carrying me up two flights of stairs but stopped short of laying me in my actual bed to teach me a lesson.

While I'm certain I acquired a terrible kink in my neck, I regret nothing. In fact, I would do it all over again for the glory— albeit temporary—of not being afraid to hold my own and securing my spot 'til the bitter end. You gotta take your wins however they come. By now, you're either heavily judging or hysterically laughing at my family. Both are fine. But when are you gonna start judging your response to fear in your own life?

Fear sucks, and while it seems crippling in the moment, it's really just you having anxiety over something that hasn't happened yet, and 95 percent of the time, that something will never happen. I've heard fear described as False Evidence Appearing Real. It's a smokescreen, like in *The Wizard of Oz*. You remember when Dorothy and crew discovered that the Wizard was just some dusty old man behind a curtain? He had no real power but had everyone fooled with sound equipment and visual effects. That's what fear is. It holds you hostage, clouds your judgment, and cockblocks your progress.

Compared to regret, fear is more like food poisoning. It'll make you feel sick to your stomach and have you searching for the nearest bathroom, too afraid to face the impending doom you've magnificently concocted in your mind. You'd give anything for the moment to pass so you can get back to feeling like yourself again, ready and energized to face the days ahead. That's fear. Its symptoms are temporary. The more you outsmart it, the more it releases its grip on you.

Regret, on the other hand, is a whole'notha heaux. It's the fear that you allowed to take root and stop the momentum of reaching your goals. If fear is food poisoning, then regret is herpes because it never really leaves you. Sure, you can suppress it for some time, but eventually it'll flare up when you least expect it. An outbreak looks like anger, frustration, or even depression over seeing other people receiving blessings that they didn't let fear stop.

> Fear holds you hostage, clouds your judgment, and cockblocks your progress.

You resent anyone living out their wildest dreams while you're still stuck, paralyzed by excuses, logic, risk assessments, and anything else you used to convince yourself not to bet on yourself. Similar to herpes, there are steps you can take to prevent future flare-ups, like going to therapy, finding another job, or entering a new relationship. But deep down, lying dormant, is the pungent realization that *you* kept *you* from an amazing opportunity, and that's a guilt that never really goes away. That's regret. She don't care about your feelings and she'll ruin all your plans every time she shows up.

What has gotten me the furthest in life and in my career has been this fundamental principle: I hate regret more than I hate fear.

Dassit. Full stop. Period. The end.

That doesn't mean I'm not constantly battling fear. I do. Often. Matta'fact, I've thought about quitting comedy too many times to count, but I don't. At the heart of the issue is the fear that, one day, I won't be funny anymore. But you know what I do until that day comes…BE FUNNY. I think God knew that the first time I performed comedy, I *had* to succeed. Most comics bomb their first time out and that thrill of redemption is what keeps them getting back onstage. That couldn't have been my testimony. I would've quit on the spot.

After building my confidence with a few wins, I did eventually bomb, and it. was. bad. People didn't bother booing, they just ordered more drinks…loudly. I got the message. Later that night, in a fury of embarrassment and anger, I told God He could keep His stupid jokes, and His stupid comedy clubs with their stupid guests and He was like, *"Everybody calm down. One bad night does not dictate your destiny."*

I was about to use fear as a scapegoat to forfeit my future. I wish I could say that was a onetime thing, but it's happened on several other occasions. I'll never forget the time I was shooting a movie in Atlanta, and I hit up my agent to book a gig in town. I figured a cool fifteen-minute spot in a new market would be a good look. A couple days later, Heidi hit me back to let me know she'd secured a gig alright. Not for the fifteen minutes I'd asked for, but for my first hour-long set… as a headliner. MA'AM! That was NOT at all what we discussed. Once again, something that should've been so simple turned into another opportunity for Jesus to bamboozle me.

I hate regret more than I hate fear.

My stomach dropped at the thought of being onstage for that long. *"I'm not ready for an entire hour,"* I convinced myself and threw several excuses at Heidi as to why we should back out, but all she said was, *"Let's just try it and see how it goes. If nothing else, it'll let you know where you stand as a performer and we can adjust accordingly."* That was easy for her to say. She wouldn't be the one catching all the L's and being dragged on the innanets if it went badly. Even though I was petrified, there's something powerful about someone else seeing more for you than you see for yourself, so I let her go through with the booking.

What scared me the most was the fact that she was actually giving me the freedom to fail. As a Nigerian, I was rarely afforded si a luxury. I'd been conditioned to strive to be the best at everythii g i tried. If I failed, that meant that something was inherently wrong with me. There was no grace given for falling short, and my perfectionist tendencies struggled to accept "a good effort." (Don't worry, I'm unpacking all'a this in therapy.)

As devastating as it might sound to my fellow perfectionists, failure is actually a perfect breeding ground for growth. When I failed organic chemistry, it liberated me to ignite other passions. You, too, can liberate yourselves by realizing that none of us are perfect. If we were, Jesus would be out of a job. Give yourself some grace. You might actually get it right by getting it wrong.

Back in Atlanta, I wasn't quite ready to take my own advice. Not only was I afraid of not having enough material to last a full hour, I also wasn't sure that I had enough pull to get 350

> None of us are perfect. If we were, Jesus would be out of a job.

people to spend their hard-earned money to see me perform. What if nobody showed up? Maybe that was my exit strategy. If ticket sales went poorly, then the show would automatically get canceled and there'd be nothing to worry about!

Except that the show sold out in a matter of days.

Heidi called elated, asking if I wanted to add a second show. MA'AM, NO. I appreciated her believing in me and all, but she really had to relax. Everything was happening so fast, and now, there was no getting out of it. Still I didn't think I was ready. So the night of the show, I padded the lineup with guest performers to kill as much time onstage as possible. I threw on a host, an opener, and even my friend, Lil Rel, who was also in town filming. But the crowd was there to see *me*. I couldn't stall much longer.

Right before I went up, the host asked if I wanted to get the wrap up light at fifty minutes and I laughed that he thought I would actually need that long. I gave myself thirty-five to forty minutes TOPS. But, as soon as I grabbed the mic, I became a beast. It was a total out-of-body experience. The crowd was electric, my jokes were hitting, and everybody was having an amazing time. I got offstage feeling on top of the world after doing what I thought was a solid half-hour set.

Except it wasn't a half hour. It was an hour and five minutes.

Yup, the girl who was afraid to take the booking, who was so unsure of her ability to deliver, had *over*delivered. As a result, the club owner gave me an open invitation to return anytime I was in town.

Leaning into fear and tackling that show head-on was batting practice for the new levels of bamboozlement Jesus would throw my way. Like the time I was booked to perform five shows in three nights, after the holidays, in the middle of a snowstorm. One sold-out show at a low-stakes venue was one thing, but performing five at Caroline's on Broadway—New York's premier comedy club—was an entirely different animal. I used to pass Caroline's in my early days in NY, and would stop to admire the marquee, believing that one day, I'd be good enough to have top billing and see my name in the lights.

Well, that day came, and it brought with it a crap ton of anxiety. Why had I agreed to perform the first week of January? People had spent all their money on the holidays. They weren't thinking about jokes. And it was winter. In New York. A blizzard was literally passing through. Things were *not* looking great, and as much as we pushed, the club refused to cancel the shows. In Atlanta, my fear was not having anything to say; now it was not having anyone to say it to. *I guess you're not as popular as you thought you were. You're not gonna be able to post a "sold out" flyer on the Gram now. Everyone will know the shows didn't do well. I don't know why you thought you could even do this.* My thoughts were having a field day in panic mode.

Most fears are birthed from our own insecurities. They prey on our weakness and feast on the lies we tell ourselves. I'm not surprised that God used the possibility of rejection—the thing I feared the most from years of bullying and people-pleasing—as a catalyst for my career. He knew that if I could get past worrying over whether or not I was enough or if people liked me, or thought I was funny, then I could get to the joy of actually spreading joy. While my thoughts spiraled, Jesus swooped in once again to show me what I'm tryna tell you: Risking it is far better than regretting it.

Not only did the show go on, but I ended up selling out all five of them—did I mention in the middle of a snowstorm. At the end of the run, the club's marketing guy told me that no matter who they scheduled the week after New Year's, it was always an epic fail. In his twenty-five years of marketing, my dates were the first time all shows had sold out...and during a blizzard, no less. I'm pretty sure he meant that as a compliment, but all I could think was, *So y'all purposely gave me the worst spot for my first time at this club? Basically, you were setting me up to fail!* No matter what their intentions were, God always intended for me to succeed. Only, His version of success looked daunting and intimidating, and I initially wanted no part of it.

It's a good thing I pushed through, tho, 'cuz from that first Atlanta show, building a one-hour set led me to open up for Chris Rock at Barclay Center in front of 19,000 fans, selling out shows in London, performing in Ireland, South Africa, and of course, shooting my first HBO comedy special. It's crazy to think that all these moments were activated by leaning into a "Let's just try it." Can you imagine the deep levels of regret I would have right now if I never did? I can't. And I honestly don't want to.

When God is pushing you out of your comfort zone and you're tempted to resist, ask yourself, "What's the worst that could happen if I go for it?" Then go for it anyway. That's what four lepers in Da Good Book did as they weighed their options for survival in the middle of a famine. The four men reasoned that if they remained outside the city, hunger would kill them. But if they entered the city, where they were forbidden, either their countrymen would kill them, or the rival Aramean army would kill them, make them prisoners of war, *or* possibly feed them. Either way, they had three opportunities

Risking it is far better than regretting it.

to die and one slim chance of survival. With the choices so bleak and nothing to lose, they decided to enter enemy territory where the Arameans had a stockpile of grub.

I'm sure fear was screaming at them to stay put. But when regret whispered, *"What if it would've worked out, but you never went in?"* it gave them the ammunition to run on and see what the end gon'be. When they entered the Aramean camp, to their surprise, they found it completely free of soldiers, but full of food. Little did they know that as they walked into the city, God had made their steps of faith sound like a mighty army was approaching. Fearing an ambush, the Arameans exited stage left, leaving behind all their goods. That's an outcome the lepers could never have imagined before they set out. They just knew they were tired of being stuck by both a disease and fear.

You and I are no different from those lepers. We're constantly faced with opportunities to sit it out and die slowly, or to get up and walk in the direction of promotion, purpose, and possibly danger. But when we walk by faith in the presence of fear, God orders our steps and makes every crooked path straight. That journey ain't always quick, nor is it easy. Trust me, I know. Impostor syndrome and I have been friends for longer than I care to admit. When it gets all up in my psyche, it creates this persistent fear of being exposed as a "fraud." Somehow I feel like if people came up close, they would find out who I really was. Mind you, I have no idea who "they" are, or what exactly it is that they would be finding out. But that's why fear is stupid. It speaks in hypotheticals, but has zero receipts. There's no actual evidence.

The people who tend to suffer from impostor syndrome are extremely high achievers. Go figure. We set the bar so high in our lives, but are constantly afraid of not being enough, while also adopting a ridiculous pattern of downplaying our accomplishments. Make it make sense, Jesus. There are so many books, conferences, and advice columns on how to hustle hard, work smarter, and boss up, but not enough material on how to handle the stress of success. What happens when you work so hard to attain a goal, and actually get it, but suddenly start to wonder if you're good enough to sustain it?

That was me on my first day of filming *Insecure*. I just knew they were going to recast me. I'd heard stories of actors not making it past the table reads, and even of productions spending extra money on reshoots after they'd replaced an actor. Somehow, I believed this would be my fate. Our showrunner, Prentice Penny, kept asking me to give him a different read with each take of one particular scene. *"Do it as if you're annoyed. Okay, now try it like you're hopeful. Let me see what it looks like if you're rushed."* Each time he had me adjust, I thought it was because I wasn't getting it right and he was growing frustrated with me.

As Brené Brown would say, the story I was telling myself was that I'd fooled everyone into believing I was a good actor based on the five auditions it took to book the role. Maybe I'd gotten really good at the three scenes I had to work from, but this was the big leagues now, and I had an entire script, choreographed movements, and bright lights to contend with—and clearly, I wasn't making the cut. Everyone would soon discover I was a fake, a phony, a sham.

That night, I cried myself to sleep and asked God to give me the strength to stomach the blow when it came. While I hate conflict, I'm not one to shy

> Fear is stupid. It speaks in hypotheticals, but has zero receipts.

away from confrontation, so the next day, I put my big girl pants on, pulled Prentice to the side, and told him to shoot straight with me and tell me what I was doing wrong. Confused, he told me that I wasn't doing *anything* wrong. In fact, he was pleased with my performance, but just wanted to have multiple emotions to play with while editing. SIR, I NEED YOU TO LEAD WITH THAT NEXT TIME! I was relieved, but what a mess. Fear literally had me believing I was getting fired from a job that I would eventually be Emmy-nominated for. *Triflin'*.

We gotta stay on guard 'cuz fear stays on its job. It clocks in overtime hours, and unfortunately, we're the ones cutting the checks and giving it full benefits. At some point, you gotta get sick to your stomach at the possibility of someone else living in *your* house, married to *your* boo, sitting in *your* office—all because you let fear stop you. The thought alone should make you want to vomit violently. Sure, life sometimes gives you do-overs, but sometimes it doesn't. That's the risk you take when you choose regret over fear. And yes, it is a choice. You make it every time you disqualify, discount, or discredit yourself. It's time to make your thoughts think twice about messing with you. You heard me correctly: Make your thoughts think twice. That's how scared your fear should be of your faith, and that's low-key the only cure for regret.

Make your thoughts think twice about messing with you.

PART III

The Breakthrough

CHAPTER 12

I MAY NOT WIN, BUT I ALWAYS WIN

I don't like losing. Never have. As a kid, I hated coming in last, probably because I *was* the last. I always felt like I needed an edge, so I devised clever ways to get wins in my family. One way was to save my food so I would have the last bite. True story. My brothers would often get bigger portions and leave me with the skinny slice of pizza, or the last soggy scoop of ice cream. So to stack a win, I waited. I knew they would eventually come back to the kitchen looking for seconds, and when they did, I would be there savoring the last bites of pepperoni and cheese with glee. Their crushed expressions were my silent victories.

Obviously, as an adult, I'm aware that losing is part of the game. It doesn't make me like it any better, but I've learned not to see my L's as defeats. They're just possibilities in waiting. In fact every major loss I've experienced has somehow transformed itself into a beautiful, unexpected opportunity. That's why I've concluded that although I may not win, I always win. I know that sounds like an oxymoron, but I got receipts. Like back in 2014, HBO had a writing competition where they were looking for diverse voices to groom. They were only accepting the first 200 applicants and submissions began at 5 a.m. in LA. No sweat. Who needs sleep?

My L's are not defeats. They're just possibilities in waiting.

I got up early, had my materials ready to upload, and my finger steady on the "submit" button. When the clock struck five, I said a quick prayer, hit enter, and was instantly shot back an error message. The volume of submissions from other trigger-happy writers, up at the butt-crack of dawn, had crashed the site.

Jesus wept.

I'd spent weeks reworking my script, building out the characters, and perfecting the jokes, only to be denied, not by merit, but by sheer cyber overload. It sucked. And it didn't help to get on social media to see other writers posting screenshots of their accepted submissions. I guess the site didn't crash for *everybody*. That was a serious L, and it hurt. But what I didn't realize was that a year later, I would book a show on the very same network that I couldn't even submit an application to. That's how you win, even when you don't win.

Oh, but it gets better.

Another time, I entered the Comedy Wings competition, hoping to be selected as a finalist. The winning comic would perform in front of industry professionals, receive $10,000, and get a holding deal at a major network. I swore that would be my big break, but three years in a row, the only break I got was in my heart when I received consecutive rejection letters. Once again, I sat back and watched as others advanced to the next level, while I hung on to the hope of a "one day."

Ya'll know about the "one day." "*One day*, it'll be my turn. *One day*, I'll make it too. *One day*, that'll be my name called." While it may sound like an empty, pathetic pep talk, that's actually Scripture. Galatians 6:9 encourages us not to allow ourselves to get fatigued by doing what we know to do, because, *one day*, at the right time, it will all pay off, as long as we don't give up. I know it gets hard to put your best foot forward, only to remain sidelined. But don't get tired. There is a win with your name on it, and when it finally shows up, God'll sweeten the deal.

Two years after my last rejection, I did eventually get to perform at the Comedy Wings competition, but not as a contestant, as a host. That's right, the same event I wasn't invited to was now flying me out and paying me top dollar to carry the show. I'd call that a win, with a cherry on top. Sometimes it takes hindsight to see losses as a win. It's not until all the pieces of the puzzle fall into place that all those hoops you had to jump through finally begin making sense.

On my wrists are two tattoos. One reads, "my times…your hands," to remind me to surrender my plans to God's timelines. The other says, "Naija no dey carry last," which is a slang saying in Nigeria that means, "Nigerians don't finish last." Essentially, every time I look down at my hands, I'm reminded that, with God on my side and my country at my back, I will not lose!

I like to do this thing where I personalize Scripture verses where God has made a promise to someone. I cross their name out and insert mine over it, because when God declares a win, He's not stingy with it. It applies to anyone who has the faith to believe it for themselves. My version of 1 Samuel 3:11 reads, *"See, I'm about to do something in Yvonne that will make the ears of everyone who hears of it tingle."* And you know what? God's kept that promise several times.

Like the time I met Oprah.

I thought that would get your attention.

It all came together after I released the trailer for *FirstGen*. I told my team that I wanted a well-known Nigerian actor to add their clout to our efforts in hopes of getting the show sold. After cold-calling a few managers, David Oyelowo was the one who showed the most interest in the project. Having worked mostly in the movie space, he didn't have much experience producing content for television, so he reached out to his vast network for guidance.

One day, he called me, excited, telling me that he'd shown the trailer to his mum and it really resonated with her. I thought it was cool that Mrs. Oyelowo found my work entertaining. After all, the goal was for people like her to feel seen and represented, but I didn't understand how his mum could move the needle on our project. That's when David said:

"And by my mum, I mean Oprah."

Come again?! (Sidebar: Did y'all peep the light flex David hit me with? So, we just out here calling Oprah "mum?" Goootit.) But, I couldn't believe it, Oprah Winfrey had seen my trailer and *liked* it? And not only that, she was interested in having me come in to pitch the show. What world was I living in? Lemme put this moment into context for you: Seven months prior, I had my breakdown on Sunset Boulevard and was close to quitting, and three months before this, I'd struggled to get the financing to even shoot the trailer. Now I was being told that the Queen Mother herself desired an audience with me? I was practically the living embodiment of Proverbs 22:29: "Do you see a man skillful and experienced in his work? He will stand [in honor] before kings; he will not stand before…obscure men" (AMP). All of my resilience, effort, and faith had culminated in this magnificent moment!

But here's how I know God has a sense of humor. The day I went into Oprah's offices, I checked my bank account and couldn't help but chuckle at what I saw. In a few minutes, I'd be pitching my show to the first Black female billionaire, and I had a whopping sixty-two cents to my name. If that ain't being bamboozled, I don't know what is. I arrived at the OWN offices and was immediately greeted with life-size images of Lady O and other prominent figures plastered all over the walls and on TV screens.

This was really happening.

To set the tone, my team and I decided to bring jollof rice from a local Nigerian restaurant, because: details. Oprah was incredibly impressed by it all. Afterward, pictures were taken and laughter was shared. Everyone went home in awe. And then came the hard part: waiting.

A few weeks later, I got the news from David that OWN had decided to pass on our show. They loved the idea, but at the time, our show didn't fit within their current programming schedule. I know it should've been a consolation prize that they liked the pitch, but the whole thing honestly felt like a sucker punch to the gut. I was so sure that all the hard work that had been put in would've sealed the deal, but now, nothing. As I was about to hang up and dissolve into a ball of tears, I heard David say, "*But…*"

But, God, don't play with me.

But, Jesus, take the wheel.

"But Oprah has decided to put her resources behind your project anyway and come on board as an executive producer."

You gotta be kidding me. How was this even possible? You have to understand: This was *pre-Insecure*. I was a "no-name somebody" that Oprah didn't have to take a chance on, but here she was, going against her own network to make my dreams come true. Tears and hyperventilation took over my body. David must've sensed my awe when he said, *"I gotta be honest, Yvonne. I've brought many projects her way, and she's never done this before."*

Again, I say, how was this even possible?

He explained that she was really passionate about her girls' school in South Africa and felt that a show like *FirstGen* could be exactly the kind of positive representation that her "daughters" should be exposed to. While this wasn't an outcome I could've predicted in my wildest dreams, this is the kind of stuff God relishes in orchestrating—not only in my life, but also in yours. After five long years of trying to get the show sold (and receiving several "no's"), I'm excited to share that we've finally found a home with the Disney+ family!

Here's the crazy part: Disney+ didn't even exist when we started trying to sell the show. But here they were, all these years later, looking for the same diverse family content that we were supplying. To make the moment even more magical, the day it was announced that *Insecure* would be ending after five seasons was the same day it was announced, after five years of praying, hoping, and a wishing, that Disney+ would be developing *FirstGen*. Even when it looks like you've lost, remind yourself that you always win.

I had to tap into that same energy the night of the 2020 Emmys.

After four seasons, *Insecure* was finally nominated for best comedy and I received my first best supporting actress nod. You wanna talk about getting bamboozled? My nomination came after a season where my character, Molly, and me to some extent, were personally *draaaaaged* and vilified all over social media. I guess God saw fit that an Emmy nom would be our redemption song. The night of the big event, surrounded by a handful of friends, we watched as *Schitt's Creek* swept every single award in the comedy category. *Every. Single. One.*

While obviously a win would have been monumental, I actually didn't feel so horrible not bringing home the gold. For the entirety of my career, I will forever be known as "Emmy-nominated actress Yvonne Orji." That's a feat not too many actresses, especially those of color, have achieved, and I managed to do it in only four short years in the game. The nomination alone drew more eyes from executives and producers desiring to work with me. Not to mention, my rate went up (#SecuringAllBags)! So while it was a loss, I surely didn't lose.

As I reflected on the *Schitt's Creek* sweep, I thought about the five seasons they had endured in relative obscurity. They'd been airing on a local station in Canada until they got worldwide distribution on Netflix leading into their sixth and final season. For six years, they'd shown up, worked hard, produced scripts, performed excellently, and for five of those six years, they got nothing. They flew under the radar and were prepared to hang it all up until a mainstream network and a global pandemic brought them directly into the homes of millions. The show that had felt like a loss to everyone except the creative team went on to *win* in front of everyone and a bunch of other creatives. And I can't e'en be mad at it. If God could do that for them, then when He does it for me, I bet'not hear any yappin' from anybody!

In Da Good Book, the prostitute Rahab had firsthand experience with losing but winning. By all accounts, she wasn't the most respected member of society. As a known prostitute, you gotta imagine the shame her profession brought her family. Walking down the street, I'm sure she got stank looks from wives who suspected her of sleeping with their husbands. Rahab didn't know how her life was gonna turn out, and while she used her body as a means for survival, she was a fighter and knew she was destined for more.

The city of Jericho, where she lived, was about to be attacked by Joshua and the Israelite army. Rahab had heard all about how God protected the Israelites and defeated their enemies, so she had to think quickly on how to turn an impending loss into a secured win for herself. When Joshua sent spies into the city, it was Rahab who took them in, hid them, and lied to the king about their whereabouts. But Rahab was no dummy. She knew how to seize an opportunity and had ample experience getting exactly what she wanted from men.

In exchange for helping the spies, her only request was that they not hurt her or her family when they destroyed the city. The spies pinky-swore on it, and when the Israelites attacked Jericho, they demolished everything and everyone in it, except for Rahab and her peoples. Even though she was deemed insignificant and counted out by her peers, in a single moment, Rahab's actions secured her legacy while everyone else took an L in the worst way.

When you think about it, Rahab was actually the perfect person to hide the spies. Her neighbors were used to seeing strange men coming in and out of her condo. They probably assumed she was conducting business as usual. No one would've considered for a second that a prostitute would be striking a lifesaving deal.

Nobody but God, that is.

He uses everything you are to get you to your wins, and everything you are has been shaped by every loss you've experienced. Inevitably, what constitutes a win for you will look vastly different than what counts as a win for me, so there's no need to compare trophies. Da Good Book says… "In a race, all the runners run…[but we should] run in such a way as to get the prize" (1 Cor. 9:24 NIV). Your prize could be making it to see another day or not cussing out that coworker who stays testing you. That counts, fam. You're crushing it! So celebrate your wins no matter how big or small they seem.

When I was barely getting by, my goal for an entire year was to not get an overdraft fee from my bank. Nothing more, nothing less. Accomplishing that would mean that I'd made enough money to cover all my needs for the year. When December 31st rolled around and I saw that the bank never got an unnecessary $35 from me, I sure as heck did a bodyroll and a Harlem shake! I'd earned it.

I hope it makes you fail better to hear about some of my losses that were turned into wins. You read that right. I hope you *fail* better. I really do. If you allow them to, some of your hardest failures will produce better wins than some of your easiest victories. So cheers to the setbacks. Raise a glass to the defeats. They may have taken you down, but they'll never take you out. Get back up and start running again. The race has been rigged. The fight has been fixed, and the outcome is: YOU WIN!

I hope you fail better.

CHAPTER 13

THE WAY UP
IS DOWN

I loved visiting my mom at work at Howard University Hospital. Walking down the long, sterilized hallways, I felt connected to her importance. She was a nurse who knew doctors and med students, and by default, I was the daughter of the nurse who knew doctors and med students. I beamed as I watched her casually converse with the head of surgery, but almost immediately got confused as I watched a friendly exchange between her and one of the janitorial staff. Even in my youth, I understood that one of these was not like the other. That's when my mom pulled me aside and taught me the secret to her success in work and in life: Treat everyone kindly because you never know if you're entertaining angels. That attitude of service, regardless of status, has guided me well into success.

In my six years of working on *Insecure*, I've never been on set trying to be number one. That position's already taken. Issa's first on the call sheet and I'm second, and I play my position like a shortstop. Every chance I get, I remind Issa, through my actions, that I'm here to serve *her* vision. It's not uncommon for me to roll up on her like, *"Gurl, you good? Whatchyu need? Have you eaten? Want me to fix you a plate? You need to take a power nap?"* Yes, she has assistants and reps on hand to tend to her needs, but while I'm around her, I choose to serve in this capacity, unasked and unexpected, because I understand the larger exchange at play. One day, I, too, will have my own show, and how I serve Issa is a direct reflection of how somebody else will eventually be of service to me. It's the Golden Rule in action. I'm doing unto her what I hope will be done unto me.

I remember when we were shooting the pilot episode and she nonchalantly said, *"I wish I had socks. My feet are cold."* I asked if she wanted me to get her some, and in true Issa fashion, she brushed it off and told me not to worry. She really isn't one to bother anybody, even at the expense of her own comfort. When we got a break in shooting, I discreetly went to the folks in the costume department and asked if they could bring her socks, and they immediately scrambled to make it happen. It would have been very easy for me to dismiss her request as "no big deal" and think, *If she ain't trippin', then I not trippin'. My feet are juuuust fine.* But I'm not on the show just to memorize lines and give a dope performance—that's my job. My *mission* is to be a value-add in every space I occupy.

It's funny how eerrybody wants to lead, but few people find satisfaction in serving. Apparently that sounds too much like being a follower, and the only thing celebrated on the 'Gram and in our group chats is to "be a BAWSE!" But people forget

> My mission is to be a value-add in every space I occupy.

that the "boss" was once an employee who followed orders. As someone who's busted my balls for years to accomplish the things I have, I'm often amazed by the "popcorn mentality," where folks honestly believe that they can jump from assistant to CEO in five heartbeats, but there's levels to this.

In Da Good Book, Elisha served as the prophet Elijah's apprentice for roughly seven years before becoming a prophet himself. That's seven years *before* the talk of a promotion even came up! Some folks work for three months and get mad when nobody notices "all of their effort." Suddenly, they wanna leave and take their talents to Miami like they're the LeBron of their industry. Well, go on and leave then. You're only taking the same you everywhere you go. And how's that working out?

Exactly.

We all got a little Orville Redenbacher in us that wants to get hot fast and pop quick, but the reality is, most times, the way up is down. In order to get to the top, you might have to start at the bottom. But if you think the bottom is beneath you, then you're not about this life. Remember, Jesus was second only to God and high-key, *was* God, yet He still humbled Himself to the point of washing His disciples' feet. I don't know about you, but I'd say that being COO of Heaven should exempt you from stooping down low to wash another man's feet, but that's where Jesus was. So remind me again why you can't roll up your sleeves to do some dirty work?

Even in that low position, Jesus still held the most power. Serving didn't undermine His influence; it actually heightened it—just like looking out for Issa doesn't diminish my worth. If anything, it shows God that since I can be trusted in this capacity, He can trust me at the next level of my purpose. That's how He used a volunteer opportunity and turned it into a master class, which turned into a job.

After interning in the writer's room for *Love That Girl!* in 2011, I moved back to NY, but stayed in contact with Stacey, the show's executive producer. I would often check in to see if she had any job leads, and one day she kept it real and suggested that I bite the bullet and move to LA. Her reasoning was that, if she did have a gig lined up, in the six hours it would take me to fly to LA, the gig would be gone. I knew she was right, so I nervously made the move in the spring of 2012.

If you think the bottom is beneath you, then you're not about this life.

Around this time, Bentley and Stacey were holding workshops to assist writers in succeeding in the writer's room. I offered to volunteer, and of course they jumped at the prospect of good, free labor (because: *who wouldn't?*). My job was to help with registration, and in exchange, I got to be in the room during the workshop, soaking up knowledge from veterans in the business and meeting writers at all levels. Toward the end of the day, Bentley called me to the front and said that since I'd been around them for a while, he wanted to see if I'd been paying any attention. I had no clue what he was talking about, but I immediately started sweating.

In front of everyone, he said that if I could pitch them a story for *Love That Girl!* that hadn't been done yet, he'd hire me to write the script. Lissen, I appreciate a good challenge, but not like *that*. I was terrified of failing this impromptu pop quiz, especially in front of a roomful of professional writers. They did this for a living. I was only an intern-turned-volunteer. What did I know? Thankfully, the crowd, who'd seen me hustling all day, was visibly rooting for me. I gave my pitch, fumbling my way through something halfway coherent. When I'd finished, Bentley took a long, dramatic pause, then nodded his head and said, "I'll buy that." The room erupted in cheers and I felt like a hometown hero.

As quickly as the moment came, it passed, and I went back to serving in the back. A few months after the workshop, Bentley not only made good on the script he'd promised, but in addition, offered me a full-time position in the writers room the following season. Through serving, I went from unpaid intern, to unpaid volunteer, to full-time staff *and* got a writing credit. God out here showing off!

Even though some of your best breaks will come from what you give, *how* you give is equally important. Da Good Book warns against doing the bare minimum just to get by. Instead, it challenges us to do our very best, as if we're working for God, confident that when we do, we'll be paid in full.[1] Bentley promoted me because he noticed the energy I brought to the company. I wasn't doing shoddy work or phoning it in. I was showing up and taking ownership of every task like it was my company. As a result, I got a direct deposit of blessings thrown my way.

> Your come up could be camouflaged as grunt work and thankless tasks.

Neither the script nor the job were in the cards when I volunteered to serve. I just did, and it paid off. Your come up could be camouflaged as grunt work and thankless tasks. Don't miss out on your next big thing because you're only focused on what an opportunity can produce in the moment. That's hustling

---

1. See Colossians 3:23–24.

backward. You'll never know an opportunity's true potential until you're deep in it or it's long gone.

There's a story in DGB where Jesus asks a woman at a well to get Him some water. Unaware of who Jesus is, the woman hesitates to do so, and He tells her, "If you only knew who was talking to you, you would be asking *Me* for a drink." What would you do differently if you only knew? Unfortunately, you *don't* always know how one random conversation can lead to the job of your dreams or how offering a helping hand can connect you to your destiny. That's why you can't only do the things that guarantee a return. Instead, do the things that'll guarantee you return to the minds of people when they think of someone kind, hardworking, generous, and willing to go the extra mile.

What you make happen for others, God will make happen for you. He'll cause somebody, somewhere to use their power, ability, and influence on your behalf. There's no telling where that source might come from, but with God at the control station, the possibilities are endless. Just ask Ruth. In Da Good Book, she went from being a broke widow, to the wife of a handsome millionaire named Boaz. Only before any of that happened, she was a caregiver to her disgruntled mother-in-law, Naomi.

> *What you make happen for others, God will make happen for you.*

Naomi had seen better days. Her husband and two sons had just died, and she'd resigned herself to being lonely and depressed for the rest of her life. She told Ruth and her other daughter-in-law, Orpah, to leave and go find new husbands. Orpah was like, *"You ain't gotta tell me twice,"* and dipped out. We don't know what happened to her afterward. Her story ended when she left. But Ruth was different. She chose to stay and care for Naomi, with no apparent benefits in sight, and ended up with a whole entire book of the Bible dedicated to her.

It wasn't an easy task to love Naomi, let alone serve her. She'd grown bitter, hopeless, and toxic. But Ruth stood her ground, telling Naomi unequivocally, "Where you go I will go, and where you stay I will stay. Your people will be my people and your God my God."[2] Her decision to stick with Naomi when it wasn't popular didn't go unnoticed, as it seldom ever does. One day, when Ruth went to gather grain, she caught the attention of Boaz, a rich, handsome landowner. He'd heard about her sacrifices for Naomi and allowed her to take as much grain as she wanted from his fields.

Now, Naomi might've been old, but she wasn't blind. She saw the bushels of grain Ruth was coming home with and picked up on the game: Boaz was tryna to shoot his shot. So Naomi helped Ruth get her swag back so she could get her freak on. Eventually, Ruth and Boaz got married, and the field where she once worked, she now owned. Ruth's story is very similar to how I landed my first manager—except that before I was his client, I was his kids' babysitter.

What had happened was, I got reconnected to one of my favorite GW professors, Dr. Skolnik, who then connected me to his nephew, Jacob, who just happened to be an executive at a major studio. For a few weeks, Jacob and I struggled to find a good time to link. His earliest availability was months out, since work kept him busy and a newborn at home kept him tired.

Where others would've accepted the off-timing of it all, I instead

2. Ruth 1:16 NIV.

saw an opportunity to meet a need. I was volunteering in the nursery at my church, and I told Jacob that if he and his wife ever needed a night off, I'd be more than happy to watch the kids. Almost immediately, his earliest availability opened up, and before I knew it, I became their regular Tuesday night babysitter.

Sure, you could see this as just another frivolous gig, but what you'd be missing was how every Tuesday night turned into an executive coaching session. When Jacob returned home, he'd school me in the ways of the industry, and while I was still babysitting for him, my career started taking off. Soon after, he decided to transition into management. The day I booked *Insecure* was also his first day at his management company. After exchanging several oh-my-goshes, Jacob asked, "So does that mean you're my first client?" and I replied, "I think so."

The seeds you sow today will grow into the tree you'll eat from tomorrow. So don't look down at your humble beginnings, just follow Jesus' 12-step plan to success, and you'll be straight. All throughout Da Good Book, Jesus was dropping major keys on how to actually get ahead in life. You wanna be first? Perfect. He says, "[The] first must be the very last, and the servant of all."[3] You want to be great? No problem. "Whoever wants to become great among you must be your servant."[4] He even suggested that on our dying day, the goal is to hear God say, "Well done, good and faithful servant!"[5] Not *friend*, not believer, but *servant*. Make no mistake,

The seeds you sow today will grow into the tree you'll eat from tomorrow.

---

3. Mark 9:35 NIV.
4. Matthew 20:26 NIV.
5. Matthew 25:21 NIV.

this approach to success will definitely require you to do the unsexy work—the stuff that doesn't have a spotlight on it, the stuff everybody secretly wishes someone else would do. But you do it. You be the one to take the initiative before the question is even asked. You come in early and leave late, when no one's watching, because the reality is, someone's always watching and taking note.

When God Himself is curating your résumé and orchestrating your good breaks, you can trust that when you stoop down to help someone else rise, you won't be overlooked, you won't get stuck at the bottom. You can relish the opportunity to be number one at playing second fiddle. There's a power in that, and that power has nothing to do with a position, but everything to do with a posture.

CHAPTER 14

YOUR WORKING OF IT DOESN'T MAKE YOU MORE WORTHY OF IT

I had just landed at London's Heathrow Airport and realized I'd forgotten my favorite pair of headphones on the plane. I found the nearest help desk, and as I waited in line to speak to the rep, I couldn't help but overhear the woman in front of me sobbing hysterically. She'd missed her flight and unfortunately it was the last one out that day. When the representative said her name, I instantly recognized it as being Nigerian. I didn't know what the issue was, but she kept repeating through hiccupped tears, *"You don't understand, it's my mom. I'm worried about my mom."* Immediately, I started praying in tongues. The rep might not have been able to help her, but this sounded like a job for Jesus.

Figuring that the only way *I* could help the situation was to pray with her, I pulled the young woman to the side, and tried to calm her. She shared that her mom had suddenly fallen ill and had been taken to a hospital in Lagos. She was worried that things could take a turn before she arrived. Thinking quickly, I messaged my sister-in-law, Tope, who's a doctor in Lagos, and asked if she knew anyone who worked at that hospital. To everyone's surprise, but Jesus', Tope knew the general manager of said hospital and reached out to him to have his staff check on the mother. The woman's spirit instantly relaxed, knowing that she had an advocate for her mom on the ground.

There I was, thinking I was coming to the help desk to find my headphones, but what I found instead was God's favor at work. You can chalk that up to serendipity if you want, but what are the odds that at the exact moment I land in London, I lose something important to me that prompts me to go to the exact kiosk where there's a woman in need. And that woman just happens to be Nigerian, who also happens to have a mother in a hospital that my newly inherited sister-in-law just happened to know the GM of. That ain't nobody's coincidence; that's the unexplainable, undeniable, unfathomable favor of God.

> That ain't nobody's coincidence; that's the unexplainable, undeniable, unfathomable favor of God.

Favor is a free gift from Heaven that can override the natural order of things. There are no gimmicks or hidden fees associated with it. You can't work for it or pay for it. All you gotta do is receive it. Like what happened at the airport, favor can cause people to go out of their way to be good to you. It doesn't need a reason and it definitely isn't merit-based. One moment of favor can catapult you further and faster than a lifetime of labor. God's favor has propelled me from intern to series regular, from barely making rent to homeowner, from almost giving up on Sunset Boulevard to being on billboards on the Sunset Boulevard—so nah, you can't tell me His favor ain't real.

I realize favor sounds like a contradiction to what I shared in the chapter "The Way Up Is Down," but it's not a contradiction, it's an exception. Hard work, delivering on excellence, and having a servant's heart will always take you far in life, but favor is its own subcategory. It has its own set of rules that can't be explained or questioned. Simply put, it's God's preferential treatment. I prefer the British spelling of "*favour,*" because it includes the letter "*u.*" I was taught the reason being was that God's favour always has "*u*" in mind. Here's how ridiculous favour is: Da Good Book says that God'll make you so poppin', you'll summon nations you've never even heard of, and nations that don't know who you are will come running after you.[1] Basically, people you don't even know to check for will actually be checking for you! That's exactly how I ended up opening for Chris Rock on his tour.

I couldn't have manufactured it if I tried. That was a rare opportunity I didn't ask for. Heck, I didn't even pray for. How could I have, when I didn't even know it was an option? But favour will cause your name to be spoken in rooms that your feet have yet to enter. I got to meet Chris from a comedy show I did where he wasn't in attendance. You read that right. He wasn't there. But you know who was? Favour,

> Favour will cause your name to be spoken in rooms that your feet have yet to enter.

in the form of Megalyn Echikunwoke—a fellow Nigerian-American actress and Chris's girlfriend at the time. I didn't know her personally but we'd met in passing at a few events and bonded over our Nigerianness. Our mutual friend, Mike Jackson, had invited her to see my performance, and after the show, we shared a few laughs and went on our merry way.

Later that night, Megalyn tagged Chris in a comment on my Instagram page, saying, "@YvonneOrji when are you gonna open up for @ChrisRock!! You are needed on the #TotalBlackoutTour." My first thought was, *Holy smokes, Batman, Chris Rock knows who I am!* I commented back, "#ComedyGoals. @ChrisRock is such a legend that I'm humbled to even be on the same post as him," and left it at that. But deep down, favour had already been activated. I couldn't unread what I'd just read. To no one but myself, I said, "Do what only You can do, Jesus." Chris never responded to the thread and I put the moment in the back of my mind.

CUT TO: Two weeks later, I was speaking at a conference in Miami when Mike called and asked if it was cool to share my number with Megalyn. She and Chris were also in Miami, and she'd seen from my Instastories that I was in town and wanted me to have dinner with them. What were the odds that all of us would be in the same city at the same time, two weeks after she'd put out the word for me to join the tour? That's not happenstance. That's God lining up every detail to work in your favour. You don't have to worry about FOMO, or meeting the "right" people. If God desires to get you in the room where it happens, He'll move flight plans and rearrange travel schedules to make sure you're where you're supposed to be.

The entire ride over to the restaurant, I practiced how *not* to be a blubbering fan girl. I was nervous and felt low-key uncomfortable to be in the presence of such greatness. To relax, I told myself to just be myself. He'd been Chris Rock for a long time, but he'd never met Yvonne Orji before, so it was about time to show him what he'd been missing. Sometimes you have to remind yourself that you're somebody, too, regardless of how much money, clout, or popularity you don't have.

Megalyn and I spent most of the night reminiscing about our immigrant upbringings and sharing industry stories. When Chris cracked a joke, I didn't try to out-funny one of the funniest minds in comedy. Instead, I told him I'd seen his performance on Broadway and how I'd screamed with glee when my favorite rapper, DMX, appeared in his movie *Top Five*. There were a few moments where I caught a smirk on the side of his face after something I'd said, and I celebrated those silent victories internally.

After a few hours of talking, dancing, and laughing, I headed back to the conference and marveled at how dope God was for making that moment forever a part of my history. I'd met my comedy idol and he was pretty cool and I didn't make a fool of myself. That was a win. I was so full from the experience that even if nothing else transpired from the connection, I'd be content.

CUT TO: Two weeks later, I got a call from my manager telling me that Chris wanted me to open up for him at the Fox Theatre in Atlanta during Memorial Day weekend. Me. A *whooole* me? That was

> Sometimes you have to remind yourself that you're somebody, too, regardless of how much money, clout, or popularity you don't have.

peak Blackness, and this was beyond major! Again, let me remind you, he'd never seen me perform before. Yet here he was, trusting me with an amazing opportunity, at a renowned venue, on a premium night. That kinda favour don't make no kinda sense, but it wasn't for me to try to compute. It was for me to recognize it, be grateful for it, and be humbled by it.

What's funny is, as a comic who doesn't use profanity in my sets, I was constantly told that not cursing was a disadvantage and that I would only be able to play to niche audiences in very pigeonholed circuits. I didn't pay this any mind, of course. My lack of curse words wasn't a surprise to God. If He brought me into this industry, I imagine it wasn't for me to fail on a technicality. When the same comic who'd predicted my "limitations" heard I was opening for Rock, he exclaimed, "That's dope, shawty! A win for one is a win for all." In my mind I was thinking, *Naaaw, homie. This not your win*, but I kept it classy.

The night of the show, I had one mission only, and that was to kill it. I may not have known exactly what it was that caused Chris to invite me on this Negro spiritual, but I did know that I was young, scrappy, and hungry and I was not throwing away my shot. When I hit the stage, I bodied the moment like Eminem in *8 Mile*. Backstage Chris was waiting with his arms folded and, when he saw me, nodded with approval and said, "That was funny. You're good." Mission accomplished. Again, if this had been the final stop on the Chris Rock train, I would'a been beyond grateful. My dreams were manifesting in surreal ways and God was reinforcing His plans for my life. But it wasn't over.

CUT TO: A month and a half later, I received an email asking my availability for a few more dates to join Chris on tour. My head almost exploded when I saw eight dates and cities between the Dolby Theatre in LA, Madison Square Garden Theater in New York, and Barclays Center in Brooklyn. I'm pretty sure I threw my phone clear across the room. The Dolby Theatre—where they hold the Oscars, and on my birthday too? Barclays Center—19,000-seater Barclays on the final night of the tour, in Chris's hometown? Like my dad would say in his Nigerian accent, "Jesus Christ of Nazareth!" Atlanta was one thing, but Chris was literally putting me on in the two most coveted comedy markets.

I know for certain he had a plethora of comedy friends on both coasts that he could've easily selected to share the stage with him. Instead, he chose the girl who did a good job one time in Atlanta? The same girl that other comics told her career would stall out because she chose to honor God? The *saaame* girl who got bamboozled into telling jokes in the first place?

That girl?

Darn right, that girl. And that girl is here to tell you that God's favour knows how to find you wherever you are, with whatever you have, and will pluck you out of obscurity to thrust you into His marvelous light.

One of the best illustrations of God's favour in Da Good Book has to be the story of the workers and the wages. There was a real estate developer who'd hired some day laborers to work on his property. Around 5 a.m., he got the first batch of workers and they settled on the minimum wage. He went back out at 9 a.m. and again at noon to get some more crew and they, too, settled on the same wage. At about 5 p.m., when the workday was winding down, he went back out and saw more laborers waiting to be hired. Feeling bad for their struggle, he sent them to work on his property.

When it came time to cash out, the developer started with the workers he'd hired last. They weren't expecting much pay, since they started so late in the day. Honestly, they would've been happy with a five-dollar foot-long, but the developer did them one better. He gave them a full-day's wage for less than a half-day's work. That's what favour looks like. They hadn't earned all that money. They couldn't make up for the lost time. But out of the abundance and goodness of the developer's heart, they got what others might have felt they didn't deserve.

When the workers who'd shown up bright and early at 5 a.m. saw how much the late crew made, they got hype! They assumed that if the folks who'd just gotten there received the full rate, then surely they'd be getting a lil' extra cash since they'd been grinding all day. I mean, that was only right. *Right?* See, the problem is, assumptions are the lowest form of knowledge. You set yourself up to be disappointed each time you rely on what you *assumed* to be true. So try not to make facts out of 'em.

When the boss gave the early workers the same amount he'd given the late workers, they were UUB-set—never mind the fact that they'd initially agreed to that rate. Here's where a lot of folks get tripped up. They feel like because they've been hustling their way into their destiny, and been grinding hard to achieve success, their effort should count for more and be rewarded accordingly. But their working of it doesn't make them more worthy of it. Yes, you have to put in effort, but Jesus still said His yoke was easy and His burden, light. Favour makes things light and easy.

Even though everyone has access to God's favour, not everyone will be happy for you when you tap into it. There will certainly be a few raised eyebrows and hushed whispers when favour propels you further, takes you higher, and routes you faster than the people who've been "paying their dues." But you cannot and should not apologize for it. All you can do is thank God for the divine shortcuts only He could provide. Don't get it twisted, though—just because favour causes you to sidestep protocol, it doesn't mean that you're better than anyone else. In the same way you can't work for it, you also can't take credit for it, so sit down, be humble.

What's interesting in the story of the workers and wages is that it was only when the early workers started comparing themselves with other folks that they lost sight of the good deal they'd originally struck. Comparison is an enemy of progress. It steals your joy, frustrates your grace, and robs you of your peace. I'll never forget the time I almost lost sight of the good thing God was doing in my life, because I let comparisons blindside me. Shortly after I got the deal for my HBO comedy special, the Variety Top 10 Comics to Watch list came out, and I was sad I wasn't on it. It's a coveted list that brings industry attention to the new front-runners in the comedy world. I knew a lot of people still weren't hip to the fact that I did stand-up, and I wanted that recognition.

> Assumptions are the lowest form of knowledge.

I was tripping about a list I wasn't on, despite the fact that HBO had just deemed me worthy enough to be part of an elite few to have a special on their network. Favour had made it possible for me to attain the thing that being on the list usually accomplished, without me ever needing to be on the list. I'd skipped steps, but because I was comparing wins and trying to prove myself, I wanted to run back down the ladder to hit a milestone I'd already bypassed. How silly was that, but how often do you do that in your own life?

I can't tell you why God accelerates one person ahead of another, but I can tell you that you'll drive yourself crazy trying to compare experiences and figure out the un-figure-out-able. If you keep your heart right, you'll eventually see that God is actively looking for ways to bend over backward to bless you.

In 2020, three years after I opened up for Chris, I got the opportunity to headline my own comedy tour and extend the same favour Chris showed me to another young comic. The girl who was excited to get a chance was now the boss giving someone else one. It brought me great pleasure to have my friend Chinedu Unaka be my opener on the tour. It was extra sweet, because before I gave Chinedu a shot, a decade earlier, he'd actually given me one first.

When I was still living in New York, I saw, through Chinedu's Facebook page, that he was a fellow Nigerian successfully doing comedy in LA. I sent him a message asking for advice, and he told me to hit him up whenever I moved to LA, which is exactly what I did. One night I met him at a local comedy club and he introduced me to the other comics as "his homegirl who was really funny." This man didn't know me from Adam, but him vouching for me gave me the props I needed within the comedy community and the favour I needed to perform at various shows around the city.

Chin and I grew to become close friends. When he wanted to transition into acting, I would help him with auditions, and when I needed help crafting a comedy bit, he was always there pitching ideas. When my fame rose and I started selling out comedy shows, Chin never got jealous. He was never a hater or jaded by the fact that he gave me a break as a comic, and yet I was headlining while he opened. If anything, through him showing me love, he became a benefactor of the continued favour on my life. That's why you gotta keep your heart right. You never know how the cookie will crumble.

Favour ain't fair, but it is abundant. It's available in large quantities and God desires to give it to you. In the Stock Exchange, insider trading might be illegal, but in the exchange between you and Jesus, He'll give you insider information that'll make up for lost time, and position you properly in purpose. You first have to believe that God has called you to it, then work like He's equipped you for it, then rest like He's favoured you in it.

God is actively looking for ways to bend over backward to bless you.

CHAPTER 15

PUT ME IN, COACH

You would think adversity was my love language, the way it gets me all fired up. When someone tells me "no," I power up like Captain Planet just got activated. I never accept the first "no" someone gives me, because I can't trust it. How do I know if it's a "no" because (1) they don't want to do it, (2) they don't know *how* to do it, (3) no one else has done it, or (4) it actually, genuinely *can't* be done. Very rarely is it Option 4. As far as I'm concerned, there's always another way, and I'll go down fighting until I find it. In church, I was taught to believe that "no" today doesn't mean "no" tomorrow, and if they told me "no," then I asked the wrong person.

Awhile back, I saw a $700 plane ticket to Nigeria that seemed too good to be true. I went as far as putting in my credit card info to book it, then suddenly the entire fare and flight disappeared. Lissen, $700 from DC to Nigeria is not something I'm willing to let go of easily, so I hit up customer service with the quickness. The first guy I spoke with wasn't the right one. He told me to kiss the flight good-bye 'cause there was nothing he could do.

Das cool. Please transfer me.

The next chick was the real MVP.

She found the flight, explained that it was with a third-party carrier, and admitted that she was a bit stumped by the fare. But then came my favorite seven words: "Let me see what I can do." Ohhh, I just got warm inside. After a long hold, she came back with good news. Not only was she able to secure a spot for me on the flight, but she would honor the original price. I kinda wanted to be transferred back to the first guy just to say, "So there was 'nothing you could do,' huh?" But that would'a been petty of me, and I'm above that…most days.

You're definitely gonna be hit with all types of denials, so it's important to distinguish between the sources, and know how to handle each accordingly. God Himself will Amazon Prime you a special-delivery "nah," but if it comes from Him, then just know that it has to be a necessary "no." It's above our paygrade to understand why God halts us in our tracks even when we believe that job, that house, that relationship, or that deal is the best we'll ever get. Not every "no" is meant to block your blessing. Sometimes, it's there to divert you *to* your blessing.

We often meet a stiff arm from God with tears and frantic "whys," but how come we don't question His blessings in the same way? I ain't never seen someone in tears, talkin'bout, *"All this goodness is just too much for one person, God! Why are You being so amazing to me?! For the love of You, please make it stop."* Nope, never not once heard that prayer. But somehow, the minute God shuts the door on a desire, we got

> Not every "no" is meant to block your blessing. Sometimes, it's there to divert you to your blessing.

questions. I love how Steven Furtick put it. He said, "If you can receive God's 'yes' with praise, why don't you receive God's 'no' with trust?"

I'mma let that one marinate like a rotisserie chicken.

What's probably making your booty tight right now is the fact that you just realized you owe God an apology for the way you treated Him after He shut down your plans. It's okay, He already forgave you. God's "no's" can be as basic as "Leave the party now," or as bananas as "Leave the company now." They won't always make sense, but like Nike, you gotta Just Do It!

Not all of His "no's" are created equal, though. Some are a definitive "absolutely not, don't even ask Me again," while others are a more subtle "not yet." The "not yet" season can be incredibly frustrating, because it's not like you're not good enough. It's not that you're not standing in faith. It's just that all the puzzle pieces haven't quite lined up yet. I can't tell you the number of times I've been READY! Like, "Put me in, Coach" ready, and God was like, "You might very well be ready, but the environment isn't ready for all your readiness."

In 2012, I just knew I was ready to be an actress when I moved to LA. By 2013 and 2014, I was itching for my big break. Problem was, my big break wasn't ready to be broken. In order for me to get my "yes" on *Insecure*, Issa first had to get her "no" from another production. Around 2013, she had a show in development called *I Hate L.A. Dudes*. (Un)fortunately, a year after it began, progress on the project stalled. That's when HBO swooped in and made a deal for her to develop *Insecure*. While I was busy giving God my final ultimatum on Sunset Boulevard, Issa was hard at work creating the character I would come to play in 2015.

What felt like God's denial was actually a perfectly timed divine delay. The year 2015 played to everyone's advantage. TV was changing, and there was a huge push for diversity in programming. Shows with Black leads like *Atlanta*, *Queen Sugar*, *Dear White People*, and *Insecure* were in high demand. So when Issa specified that the best friend role would also be another dark-skinned Black woman, which at the time was a rarity to see on mainstream television, HBO didn't trip at the request. You wanna know who's pretty dark-skinned? Me, that's who. What was celebrated in 2015 would not have been well received in 2013 or 2014, when I was *soooooo ready*. Through all the refusals I'd gotten, God was setting the stage for my breakthrough, and I ain't e'een know it.

If you're a doer like me, you probably lose your mind in the "not yet" seasons because they require a level of patience that we're not accustomed to. We can't help but want to *do* something—work some strategy, learn a new skill—anything that will help move the needle. But it's "peace be *still*," not "peace be *hustlin'*." Relax yo'self, boo. God doesn't need your help. He needs your participation. There's a difference. Help means that through your effort, you can make a meaningful difference. That's your ego wanting to be in control. You won't take credit for your part openly—you leave that to false humility—but deep down you relish the satisfaction of knowing that your effort had something to do with your success. That still puts you in the driver's seat and pushes Jesus out of the equation.

It's "peace be still," not "peace be hustlin'."

On the flip side, giving God your participation means that you fall back to whatever He says. You surrender to His instructions no matter how much your reasoning wants to fight against it. Recently, Holy Spirit checked me and told me that what I tried to pass off as "surrender" was really me doing things my way and asking God to put His signature on it. Eventually, after I'd strategized, worried, and over-thought myself into exhaustion, that's when I would invite Jesus into my situation for a cleanup on Aisle 5. That was wack, and definitely the opposite of "not my will but Yours."

On this particular download from Holy Spirit, I was recording what He was relaying on an app on my phone. When I thought He was done I went to press stop, but I heard Him say, *"Leave the tape open."* That could be your message for today. Leave God open to do the things eyes have not seen and ears have not heard. On the basketball court, you pass to a player that's open; well, God wants the ball. If you're tired of being sidelined, imagine how He feels riding shotgun in the affairs of your life. He's screaming, "Put Me in, Coach! You can't handle it all by yourself. I'm open."

We sing songs with lyrics that invoke God's presence and bless-ings to rain down on us, but what if we've gotten it all wrong this whole time? What if it isn't "let it rain," but rather, let it *reign*. Like, let God's power reign over you. Let His comfort reign through you. Let His peace reign inside of you. It's not water falling from the sky. It's His sovereignty ruling in your life. Reign is what kings do. So if we call Jesus the King of Kings, it's about time we let Him be King over our situations. If He's the Lord of Lords, then let's allow Him to be Lord over our worries, anxieties, and doubts. He says that His thoughts and

His ways are higher than ours, and the only way they get on the same wavelength is when we holla at Him first, *before* we create chaos in our lives.

A dude named Naaman in Da Good Book learned quick and fast that our thoughts and God's tactics are not in the same tax bracket. Naaman was rich, but he had leprosy, so that sucked. He couldn't even get a quarantine bae in his big ol' mansion. Needless to say, he was desperate and willing to drop stacks to fix his situation. Unfortunately, the solution God provided didn't fit his prototype for a cure. When the prophet Elisha prescribed him to dip seven times in the Jordan River to heal himself, Naaman felt downright disrespected. The Jordan was where gen-pop and animals bathed, so how could a man like him, with status, be expected to associate with such filth?

Naaman's problem was that he expected his bank account to elevate him to a VIP-caliber cleansing, and that's sometimes the same struggle people with resources and money have when it comes to trusting God. They rely on what their funds can afford them and forget that little is much when God's in it. Thankfully Naaman had an assistant who was able to talk some sense into him. She reasoned that if the prophet had suggested he do something extravagant, he would've done it, so, why not do the simple thing— just wash and be cleansed, bruh. Dassit. Of course, when Naaman put his pride aside, and put Jesus inside his whole situation, he got hecka bamboozled when out of the dirty Jordan, his skin became smooth as butter.

Our thoughts and God's tactics are not in the same tax bracket.

Life is guaranteed to throw a rack'a "no's" your way, but you have the audacity and the authority to push back when others try to set limitations on your expectations. However, when God Himself gives you the Dikembe Mutombo, "not in my house" finger, that's not the time to push; that's actually when you release. You surrender to His will and accept His "no" because, well…God knows.

CHAPTER 16

FOCUS ON
YOUR FOCUS

T he worst part about going to therapy is when you've stacked up
a week's worth of aggression over transgressions committed by a
partner, a parent, a friend, or a coworker, and you believe your therapist
will be an ally in your frustration, but instead, they challenge you like
you're the culprit. Asking ridiculous questions like, *"So what part do you
play in all of this?"* No, Dr. Robinson, this is not about *me*. We are here
to talk about how triflin' so-and-so is. But Dr. Robinson ain't treating
so-and-so, so all her attention is laser-focused on how you can make
better choices. Basically, Dr. Robinson just told you (read: me) to mind
yo' business, or the Nigerian equivalent, face your front, but who asked
her anyway.

I had a boss who put it another way. He would often tell me to
"focus on my focus" especially when it came to my career. His advice
was to set my vision, put my blinders on, and stay inside of my lane.
That reminds me of an after-school program I used to watch on PBS

called *The Joy of Painting*. The artist, Robert Norman Ross, was this happy-go-lucky guy who wore a button-up and rocked a big red fro. Each day, he drew trees—all types of trees: trees in the forest, snow-capped trees, trees surrounded by water. Every afternoon we knew what to expect because Bob Ross stayed in his lane and focused on his focus. No matter the season, we were gon'get a tree. Never, not once, did he deviate from his sweet spot and start drawing abstract boxes.

Similarly, there's no uncertainty that humor is my strength, and humor told through a Nigerian-American lens is my specialty—that's my "tree." No matter which way I slice my comedy, it's gonna some-how connect to my Nigerian-American upbringing. Performing comedy from this perspective is actually how Issa and I first connected. She was introduced to my work through a funny sketch video I'd posted on You-Tube. Then Senator Obama was weeks away from clinching the presi-dency, and in the video, I talked about how Africans from every country would come out of the woodwork, tryna claim him as a long-lost relative if he won. The video resonated with Issa on a personal level because her family is part Senegalese—something I didn't know at the time.

Even though we didn't know each other well, Issa and I formed an appreciation of each other's art and hustle. When I moved to LA, we supported one another as two Black girls tryna make it in these Hol-lywood streetz. The place where Issa actually saw the most potential for my funny was when I hosted an African fashion show. Not performing at any of LA's premier comedy clubs, not watching me act on anybody's TV screen, but an African fashion show. Instead of focusing on the mainstream rooms I was denied access to, I made the best of the rooms that embraced me and prepared me for what God had already prepared for me.

What's interesting is, I released that YouTube video in 2008. Issa and I officially met in 2012. Fast-forward to 2014 when I hosted the fashion show that revealed to her my range as a comic. And then in 2015, when I released the *FirstGen* trailer, that's what showed her and the producers my skills as an actress. That's a seven-year span of me drawing my own trees, focusing on my own focus and dominating what some would consider a niche market. However niche it was, leaning into my Nigerianness became exactly what was needed to grab the attention of the right person, at the right place, at the right time, and differentiated me from the rest of the pack.

Unfortunately, too many people trick off opportunities by copying what's trendy or bogarting their way prematurely into spaces, all in the name of trying to get "put on."

Speaking of which, can we pause for a sec to address the detriment of "trying"?

Now, I'm not talking about the trying that's accompanied by legit action. I'm talking about those people who talk about how they're trying *to try*. You've met them, I know you have. And if you're being completely honest, you might've even been them, or maybe you're them right now. If so, there's still time to save yourself. These are the folks you meet at a networking event, they hem you up in a corner, and talk about what they're "trying to do." They may even sweeten the delusion by adding, "I mean, it's taking me a long time because I've never seen anyone else do what I'm tryna do." They must've missed that Scripture about how there's nothing new under the sun, but hey, you do you, boo. The problem is not that they're ambitious, it's that they "try" to do so much that they never actually *do* anything. Their focus is all off.

Two whole years can go by, and I guarantee you'll see that same person "trying" to put together a business plan, or "trying" to connect with the right person who will open the right doors for them. And when they do meet that person, what will they have to offer? Definitely not a script or a reel or anything substantial, because that would be too much like work. I can't tell you how often people spend time *trying* to get five minutes to pick my brain, and when they eventually succeed, it's a hot mess of wasted energy. When I ask *how* they are trying—if they're in acting classes or writing groups—it's met with, "You know, I was gonna do that, but I wanted to see if you had any recommendations." Sir, ma'am, that's what Facebook groups were invented for. Use them.

> *The problem is not that they're ambitious, it's that they "try" to do so much that they never actually do anything.*

When I encounter these individuals, my usual response is just to smile and offer up some vague form of encouragement like, "Okay, I see you. Keep doing your thing. You got it!" But because you and I have a relationship, hear me when I say that it'll serve you better to stop tryna Hustle Man your way in, and simply focus on perfecting your craft. When Peter was about to walk on water, he didn't say, "Lord, if it's really You, command me to *try* to come to You." Nah, he just stuck his foot in the deep end and walked. So I'mo tell you like Yoda told Luke Skywalker, "Try not. Do. Or do not. There is no try."

Your future thanks you. Signed, Management.

Okay, I'm done.

By the time *Insecure* began casting, I was so completely focused on doing my own thing and making *FirstGen* a reality that I almost missed out on it. It wasn't until my former roommate ChiChi Anyanwu, a manager in New York, sent me a casting notice for the show that I realized it was really happening! Now I just needed a way to submit myself for the auditions, since I didn't have an agent or manager or even a lawyer at the time. Ain't that the bamboozlement of Jesus, though? One minute, you can feel hindered without representation, but then Jesus'll use a former roommate, three thousand miles away, to make sure you don't miss out on what's for you. Jesus be knowin'!

In total, there were five rounds of auditions for the role of Molly. I knew I wasn't the most qualified, and I often felt like I was in over my head. I had no sufficient credits to my name, but I couldn't concentrate on that. Not if I wanted a fighting chance at succeeding. What you focus on will expand, and it will either enlarge your territory or deflate your drive. The second round is where I met with the producers. To prepare, I did what I do before any major meeting with new people... Googled them. That's right, my secret weapon for success is the World Wide Web. And here's the best part: It's free.

Google is way too free for you to ever "not know." That alone should remove 95 percent of the excuses in your life. Not knowing is one thing—but not desiring to know is unacceptable. I do Google image searches so I know what everyone looks like. I read interviews to discover random facts that can be worked into casual conversation. The last thing you want is to be in a meeting and

> What you focus on will either enlarge your territory or deflate your drive.

be surprised to learn you both went to the same college. That's an epic fail.

I saw that the director, Melina Matsoukas, would be attending the audition, so I did a deep dive and discovered that she'd directed music videos for the likes of Beyoncé and Rihanna. One look at her Instagram page told me that she was fashion forward. I immediately knew that, style-wise, she'd be the one to impress, so my wardrobe game had to be on point! Problem was, Molly was a whole entire lawyer, and the way my accounts were set up, I might could pull off paralegal.

What I lacked in luxury, though, I made up for in creativity. I pulled out pieces in my closet and added specialized touches to them, like an Ankara-print pocket square to a thrift store blazer (my "tree," which became a topic of conversation). To set it off, I figured every good lawyer needed a signature briefcase. Yeah, I didn't have that either, but I did have a uniquely shaped overnight bag that I repurposed to be my briefcase. Teddy Roosevelt famously said, "Do what you can, with what you've got, where you are," and that was the best I could do with what I had, and by the grace of God, it was just gon'have to be good enough.

As I waited my turn outside the audition room, I could hear other actors going for it. One of the scenes we had to prepare was the fight scene between Issa and Molly at the end of episode one. Some actors made the choice of playing it like an all-out brawl, and I thought maybe I'd misunderstood the scene. Is that what they wanted? When you're auditioning, all you have are the choices you make with the words on the page. They won't always be right, they won't always be wrong, but they will always be *yours*. Kinda like the story of the sisters, Mary and Martha, in Da Good Book.

While Jesus was holding a connect group at their crib, Mary chose to sit at His feet and soak up every last word. Martha, on the other hand, was busy in the kitchen getting food ready for the let-out. Both positions were perfectly fine and absolutely necessary. The problem started when Martha tried to enforce her own agenda onto Mary. She wanted Jesus to scold Mary for not helping her in the kitchen (just like I be tryna get Dr. Robinson to check the folks falling short in my life), but to Martha's surprise, Jesus ended up checking her with a Brady Bunch–style "Martha, Martha, Martha," and explained that Mary had made the best choice for herself in the moment.

Nothing hurts more than being shut down by Jesus Himself. But Martha was doing what most of us do when we don't own our choices or value our value: discredit someone else's. The most valuable thing you can bring to any situation, relationship, or opportunity is your whole entire, confident, and secure self. No one can do you better than you, boo. But that also means you can't do anyone else better than them either. The minute you try to focus on someone else's focus, you've lost your magic.

When we envy what others have, we're essentially requesting a do-over with God, because apparently He didn't get it right the first time. Da Good Book says that we've all been given specialized gifts. One man may have the skills to plant, another, the talent to water what was planted. But at the end of the day, it's only God who can do da dougie on it and make the whole thing pop.[1] You can be a planter, trying your darndest to be a waterer, but if that's not your ministry, it ain't gon'work!

Your talent is not irrelevant just because someone else's gift gets more shine. You have no idea the cost of that shine nor the weight of

---

1. See 1 Corinthians 3:6.

their glow. On occasion, I've had to check myself when I've felt myself getting jealous or feeling inferior to someone else's good break. What I've discovered is that those feelings of insufficiency point back to a lack of gratitude. When we're grateful for what we have, we become content with who we are, and when we're content with who we are, we're able to show up confidently as our full selves.

At the audition, I was tempted to second-guess my initial instinct of playing the scene more irritated than angered, but I thought against it, and went with what I'd rehearsed. If it didn't work, then at least it wasn't because I'd copied someone' else's choice. My instincts ended up being right, though. When I entered the room with my jacket and "briefcase," the first thing Melina said was, "Well, look at you! Looking like you'bout to litigate." With that comment, I knew before I'd even opened my mouth that I'd left a lasting impression.

> *Your talent is not irrelevant just because someone else's gift gets more shine.*

During the fifth and final audition with the network, which is called a test (and boy, was it ever), it came down to me and two other actresses as their top choices for Molly. We all knew this would be a life-changing opportunity, and with the stakes so high, I had to believe that God wouldn't bring me this far just to bring me this far. The other two actresses were also Christians, and I thought to myself, *Deng, Jesus, I can't even play the God card 'cuz they' got it too, ugh!* We even prayed together. Clearly, Jesus was gonna get the glory one way or another, but I really wanted it to be with me.

This wasn't just a job for me. It was an assignment. So are all the platforms God places you on. They're not just cool opportunities, and you're not just there to look cute. There's someone who needs to collide with the love of God through you. That doesn't mean you gotta put extra sauce on it. Don't make it weird. All you gotta do is let the light in you shine through in how you handle situations, how you speak about others, and the general atmosphere you create when you take up space. People will see everything they need to know without you doing anything but being yourself.

When it was finally my turn to test, I was brought into a dark theater with all the executives in suits and expressionless faces. Did they forget this was a comedy? The stale environment was a drastic difference from the four previous auditions that were held in rooms drenched with natural light and hope. During a scene where I was used to receiving big laughs, the best I got were muffled chuckles, and that crushed my soul. Those are the moments where you gotta follow the advice laid out in Proverbs 4:25–26: "Keep your eyes straight ahead; ignore all sideshow distractions….and the road will stretch out smooth before you" (MSG). In other words, focus on your focus.

I still had two more scenes to go, and I told myself, "*Okay, Yvonne, pretend like you're doing a comedy show, and you might be bombing right now, but no matter what, you finish your set! You hear me? You finish and you never let'em see you sweat!*" My focus kicked into overdrive, and I eventually got through it and walked out with as much composure as I could muster. Before I even hit the door, I heard one of the suits say, "Okay, so what do we think about that one?" Deng, they could've at least waited 'til I left the room to throw me to the wolves.

I walked to my car, crying in defeat, trying to figure out what I could've done better. There was so much riding on this moment. Not to mention on my bank account. We'd already signed the contract, so I knew exactly how much I stood to make or lose, and the thought of losing had me weak. I sat in my car contemplating how to handle the bad news when it came, and I suddenly heard Holy Spirit say, *"You have no idea how I'm working behind the scenes on your behalf."* I interpreted that to mean that even if this role wasn't for me, it would lead to something else. Maybe it wasn't supposed to work out so that I could create my own show.

In an instant, I'd stopped believing the positive possibilities, and immediately fled to damage control. With my words, I was already ruling myself out, but somehow simultaneously believing for God's best. It's like that father in the Gospel of Mark who told Jesus, "I believe. Help my unbelief!" Eventually we gotta trade in whatever thoughts are leading us to dead ends for those that get us to our expected end. I walked back into the HBO offices to visit a friend and was mortified to see Issa and all the producers walking toward me. I was supposed to have been gone for almost twenty minutes, not looking like I was lurking after an audition. Of course, I received raised eyebrows, and when Issa got on the elevator without even so much as a "Good job, girl," my heart sank. I was positive then that I hadn't booked the role.

When the casting director, Vickie Thomas, also walked through the lobby area, I just wanted to evaporate into the walls. I was furious that my friend was taking so long to come down and was making me look like a deranged actress who couldn't let go of an audition. As Vickie stood waiting for the elevators, one of her associates whispered something in her ear, and she looked back at me. Again, I wanted to disappear. As the elevator doors opened and Vickie got in, she turned to me and said, "Have a good weekend. You deserve to, because you booked it." Unable to control myself, I picked up the associate who'd whispered in her ear and spun her around, before realizing she was an actual grown woman, and set her down. The elevator doors closed, and I stared at my reflection in the chrome fixture in disbelief.

This is what God meant when He said He was working behind the scenes on my behalf? I'm still in awe of that moment. My friend finally showed up and she had tears in her eyes. She'd heard the good news, too, and we both marveled at how someone with my very humble beginnings could be standing in the HBO lobby, about to be a series regular on one of their flagship shows. And to think this all started because I dared to focus on a style of comedy that wasn't always popular or profitable. But if you're only focused on what's popular, you're gonna miss out on doing what's purposeful.

> With my words, I was already ruling myself out, but somehow simultaneously believing for God's best.

PART IV

The Booked,
Blessed,
and Busy

CHAPTER 17

Don't Let Your Talent Write a Check Your Character Can't Cash

We all pray, believe, grind, and pray some more for success. Dass a fact. You're not reading these pages for the fun of it. Nah. You, too, want to get tricked into living the life of your dreams and achieve the big, bold goals you've set for yourself. However, your true motives for achieving success reveal a lot about your character, and your character will either lead you to the Promised Land, or down a landslide. Talent is what gets you on the court, but character keeps you in the game. Sadly, too many people find themselves in a position where their talent has written a check that their character can't cash. A word of advice: It's a little too late to decide the kind of person you wanna

> Talent is what gets you on the court, but character keeps you in the game.

be when you make it, while you're on the brink of making it. Your judgment gets real murky when you see the contracts, the flashing lights, and the open doors.

There's no way I could've tried to figure out my boundaries as an actress while signing a contract with more zeroes behind a number than I'd made in my entire life! But every day and in every field, people sign on the dotted line to gain fame and fortune by compromising their faith or their standards. Not you, though. Nah, you're too cool for that. In fact, you're ICE—that's a person of integrity, character, and excellence.

Personally, I think the method of attaining success is actually more important than the success itself. When Da Good Book asks what good it does for a person to gain the whole world, but lose their soul in the process,[1] it's inviting us to do a heart check on what we value. The truth is, money doesn't change people; it only magnifies what's in their hearts. If you have an addictive personality, then wealth only heightens your addictions and gives you access to even more expensive habits. If you're kinda arrogant now, when nobody but your momma knows your name, then you're bound to be a jerk of epic proportions when the spotlight shines bright on you. On the flip side, if you're the type to donate to soup kitchens, then when you glow up, you'll be an even more generous giver.

It's out of the abundance of the *heart* that the mouth speaks—not the bank account. So what's your heart saying? Don't worry, it'll

---

1. See Mark 8:36.

tell on you soon enough. Just like it snitched on King David in Da Good Book. After he defeated Goliath, David became the heavyweight champion of the world and got to marry one of King Saul's daughters. A few years later, he took the crown himself, and became king. But like many great men, before and after him, David started feeling himself, and a momentary lapse of judgment cost him his reputation and almost his life.

One day, he saw a beautiful woman named Bathsheba taking a shower and was mesmerized by the water glistening all over her bawwdyy, so he sent for her. When she arrived, he skipped all the small talk and got straight to the point like a Jodeci song, telling her, "Every freak'n night and every freak'n day, I wanna freak you, baby, in every freak'n way!" They did da nasty, and a few weeks later she hit him with that Clearblue pregnancy test.

Problem was, Bathsheba definitely had a husband, but Uriah couldn't have been the baby daddy 'cuz he was off at war. So, like a Maury Povich reveal, David was 99.9 percent the father. Instead of doing the noble thing and telling the truth, David concocted a shiesty plan. He sent for Uriah to come home from war so he could go make love to his wife. But Uriah was the epitome of an ICE person. He had too much integrity as a soldier to be enjoying time off while his fellow brethren were out getting killed on the battlefield, so he refused the offer. Faced with a new conundrum, David whipped up a problematic plan B. He wrote a letter to his top general, asking him to put Uriah on the front lines, so he could die in combat—which is exactly what happened.

In case you missed it, David—the onetime shepherd boy, turned celebrated war hero, now king—saw a woman minding her beautiful business, took her between the sheets, got her pregnant, and to cover up his tracks, had her husband killed at war. You don't need *The Real Housewives* of anywhere 'cuz the Bible got enough drama for days! One split second of not focusing on his focus caused David to abuse his power in a way that overshadowed his talent and destroyed his character.

It's the thoughts you allow to linger a moment too long, or the deal you make that's a little sketchy, or the corners you cut when you think no one will notice, that cause the checks your talent writes to bounce. Before I booked the role for Molly, Jesus and I had already had some frank conversations about what would be fair game for me and what would be deal breakers for me in the industry. Together, we decided that roles with cursing were par for the course, so I was cool with it when the scene called for it, but not in my personal life.

When it came to nudity and sex scenes, I knew this would be a bit trickier to navigate. The chances of me bypassing this area as an actress would be pretty slim, unless I wanted to stick to Hallmark movies. As someone who is waiting until her wedding night to have sex, I've often said that I want to leave some things to be discovered by my husband. Therefore, nudity isn't an option for me. Prior to signing the contract for *Insecure*, I made sure to talk with the producers about their vision for my character and joked about needing to protect my areolas because my parents were still alive and I didn't want to be written out of their will.

While I had my boundaries, I knew it would be imperative to reach a middle ground, where I could marry their vision for Molly's adventurous love life while simultaneously protecting my own personal brand. I couldn't just bulldoze my way into their offices and start making demands, talkin'bout "what I'm not gon' do!" 'cuz that's a surefire way to get fired, and also doesn't make for healthy partnerships. I had to show them I was a believable enough actress to sell the scenes, without selling myself short. Sure, there were some folks who wanted me to show more than I was comfortable with, and I had to keep using all'a my words to explain why that wasn't gon'fly.

The use of a body double was suggested but I didn't want to chance someone else showing more than I was comfortable with. Never being one to leave anything to chance, I created a four-minute sex-scene compilation video, highlighting the different scenarios I wouldn't mind forever living on the interwebs. I pulled clips from other premium cable shows and movies to show the producers the amount of wiggle room we had to work with. Nowadays, we have specialized staff on sets called intimacy coordinators who serve as liaisons between actors, directors, and the production to ensure that actors feel protected while the directors' vision is carried out, but back in 2015, I was my own advocate.

There were definitely moments where I had no clue how my desires would be received. I wondered if this would be my Esther moment where I would have to declare, "If I perish, I perish," and walk away or be recast. As heartbroken as I would've been, I knew I had to stand strong in my convictions. Success wasn't gonna be worth it if I couldn't honor God with my gifts. So, if this was the end of the road for me, then God would have to figure out what came next. Since He was the one who called me to it, He would need to be the one to walk me through it.

Eventually, the producers and I reached a happy medium. Before any intimate scenes were shot, I would speak with the director

> Success wasn't gonna be worth it if I couldn't honor God with my gifts.

about what shots and angles would be seen, wardrobe would provide modesty garments, and production made sure it was a closed set, meaning that extra monitors were turned off and only necessary crew would be allowed in the room. Everything turned out to be exactly what I needed to feel protected and what they needed to exercise their creativity.

I still get asked all the time how I could reconcile playing a character like Molly, given that I've never had sex. I sarcastically respond, "Sooo, should Denzel Washington not have played a murderous, corrupt cop in *Training Day*, given that he's never been a murderous, corrupt cop?" See how silly that sounds? Honestly, I think having me in the role actually speaks to the strategicness of God and the bamboozlement of Jesus. By placing me in a position that most Christians are wary of navigating, God is able to give you, your mama, and your cousin, too, an example of someone who's succeeding in a field that isn't homogeneous to church, yet still manages to maintain core values. That's literally what He called us to do. When He said, "Go into all the world," He didn't mean, "Go into all the Christian gatherings." We're already there.

It is interesting, though, how polarizing the subject of virginity is. I remember being asked in an interview why anyone even knows that fact about me, and my response was that if we can be okay talkin'bout throuples, then surely we can be cool discussing holding out until the wedding night. My existence shouldn't faze the woman who enjoys a vibrant sex life any more than her lifestyle should hinder mine. There is a certain level of peace that I personally enjoy with maintaining my virginity in the industry, especially as a woman in comedy.

I'm surrounded by all types of men: high-powered men, married men, you name it. Those spaces can be a lil' tricky to navigate, but I've found it particularly refreshing to not have anybody's boo calling my phone talking reckless, accusing me of crossing the line with their man. The one time that *did* happen, I was certain she had the wrong number, 'cuz, like Shaggy, it wasn't me.

It doesn't mean I haven't been hurt in the past by my decision to wait. When I first got to LA, I befriended a guy who was a more successful entertainer than I was at the time. He took me under his wing and showed me the ropes. Naturally, I was grateful for his assistance and believed that our relationship was strictly platonic. Well, one night we went out to celebrate his latest achievement, and I was thrown for a loop when he told me that every relationship functions best when both parties make compromises.

Relationship?

Who was in a relationship and what compromise you talkin'bout, Willis? It didn't take long for me to put two and two together. Apparently, even though he knew my stance on sex, and had even helped me sell merch from my T-shirt line that says "Keepin' It Locked 'Til I Get That Rock,"[2] he still somehow believed that I would like him enough to forget about a promise I made to Jesus when I was seventeen. *Wheretheydothatat?* I politely thanked him for dinner and explained how that wasn't a thing I was doing.

A few weeks went by and I noticed the distance that had grown in our friendship. Prior to that dinner, he'd invited me to an event at another celebrity's house. He thought it would be a great connection for me to make. However, the day of the event came and went without a word from him. That was painful. Was he really dangling that opportunity in hopes that I would put out? Even though he had me twisted

---

2. See www.rockyourstance.com.

to think that he held any power over my success, I still definitely cried to God that night, asking Him why everything had to boil down to the one thing that was a non-negotiable for me? I knew setting that standard wouldn't be a cakewalk, but why'd it have to hurt so bad?

Months went by without us speaking, and then one day he randomly reached out and invited me to the movies. I had forgiven him by then and Holy Spirit gave me the green light to go. When I got in the car, he handed me a hand-written card that read, "Sorry I fell out of your life when you wouldn't have sex with me." All I could do was laugh. He admitted that what he did was foul and apologized for being "that guy." We've remained cool ever since and as my star rose, he commended my ability to achieve success on my own terms.

Those terms have definitely sustained me, but I admit that on set, I've had to catch myself a time or two. If you've watched *Insecure*, you'll know that there's no shortage of fuuuyne men on our show—literally a single girl's dream. When my love scenes got more frequent, it for sure became a test of my will to see if my convictions would be easily swayed once I saw the handsome love interest they'd cast. I found myself as terrified of shooting the scenes as I was excited by them.

I'll never forget one particular day when I looked on the call sheet and got super giddy because I was acting opposite a male counterpart who shall go unnamed. Instantly, I heard Holy Spirit say, *"Whatchu getting so happy for? Oh, so you think this your cheat code to play the system, huh? So you can remain a virgin, but still get your rocks off under the guise of work? Is that what we're doing now?"*

Deeng, Holy Spirit! Let me *live!*

But He was right. Walking this walk isn't about living in the technicalities. You know the technicalities well: *"Technically, it's not cheating...technically, I'm still saved...technically, no one has to know."* All them technicals are fit'na get'chu got. Which I did. It may seem like nothing, but left unchecked, those small, seemingly insignificant thoughts and feelings could grow in a way that'll have me losing sight of my reason for being on the show in the first place.

Not letting your talent write a check that your character can't cash isn't a onetime event. It involves constantly analyzing your motives. When we're mindful of who we represent, we realize that our calling is bigger than the thing we do well and larger than any temporary feeling. In Isaiah 26:8, it says that God's name and reputation should be the desires of our hearts. That means we can't just go around operating in mediocrity— God's name is on the line. And we're not able to act unscrupulously just to get to the top—because God's reputation is at stake.

> When we're mindful of who we represent, we realize that our calling is bigger than the thing we do well and larger than any temporary feeling.

In the movie *American Gangster*, Denzel's character was adamant about upholding the quality of his product, Blue Magic. To him, it was a brand name, like Pepsi. He stood behind it. He guaranteed it. We're also gonna have to stand behind the character our talent produces. I know I've said it before, but I'll say it again: You're going to make it. Yes, *you*! You've worked too hard and prayed too long not to. But before that happens, let these words by Christine

Caine sink in: *"If the light shining on you is brighter than the light shining in you, then the light that's on you will destroy you."* God's not about to let you go out like that. He would rather delay your success than have your success derail your destiny. When you take the time to develop your character, God will do His part to develop your career—and that's a check you can take straight to the bank.

> When you take the time to develop your character, God will do His part to develop your career.

CHAPTER 18

BENTLEYS
DON'T GO ON SALE

At the 2003 MTV Video Music Awards, Chris Rock made a joke about Janet Jackson dating rapper/producer Jermaine Dupri. He thought the pairing was a bit odd, because, in his mind, Janet was a ten, whereas Dupri, he felt, was a solid four. The joke went, *"Seeing Janet Jackson with Jermaine Dupri is like finding out about a sale a day too late. It's like, '[Deng], they were selling Bentleys for $4 yesterday? I had a shot. I messed up, man!'"* While the audience laughed, the reality is that Bentleys don't go on sale. Yet every day, people discount themselves in both relationships and business.

One of my morning mantras is, "I deserve God's best." I'll marry His best, live in His best, and work with His best. Jesus died on the cross for me to get all'adat, so it would be a waste of a crucifixion to discount what was already paid in full. I once dated a guy who appeared to check off a lot of my boxes. He read books, loved Jesus, was celibate, *and* financially stable. Despite all of these qualities, before we

> Jesus died on the cross for me to get all 'adat, so it would be a waste of a crucifixion to discount what was already paid in full.

started dating, I looked him square in his eyes and said, "You're the unicorn everyone said would be impossible to meet. However, if you're not it, please exit stage left, 'cuz that means there's a 2.0 version of you out there, and I can't have you blocking my blessing."

He was shocked that I would say that, but I could be so bold in faith because I know my worth and I value what I bring to the table. Lissen, I've waited far too long for God's best to be thrown off by any counterfeits. I'm the same way in business. Awhile back, there was a major brand that approached me to be part of a campaign. They planned on pairing me with nontraditional talent but wanted to pay me at their same rate. Well, that wasn't gonna work, so I told my agent to pass on the offer. Although it was a brand that I was excited to work with, I needed to set expectations for both the company and my reps on how to properly view and value me.

I'd been in this situation before, albeit on a much smaller scale. When I used to host weddings, every time I betrayed myself by lowering my rate, I had nobody to blame but me. I ended up doing more work, but would come home with insufficient funds. I shortchanged myself because I low-key doubted that I could carry an entire event. Other times, I was just so desperate for money that anything was better than nothing. But you experience that sucky feeling of regret enough times, and you learn how much better "nothing" is on your own terms. As you're building your profile, there will be times to offer taste tests for clients to sample and get to know the brand, but after everyone's gotten hooked, set your rate!

Eventually, the brand that wanted to work with me increased their offer, and I still passed. I knew it was a gamble, but sometimes you gotta bet on yourself. After weeks of holding out, they came back a third time. This time, they more than doubled their initial offer, and I gladly accepted. When we shot the commercial and I did what I do best, one of the other cast members complimented me, saying, "Wow! You're so good at this. You're a pro!" I wanted to say, "Chick, I *does* this!" In that moment, though, I felt validated for trusting my gut and sticking it out to get what I deserved.

If I accepted everything that came my way, at whatever standard others dictated, that would be the equivalent of getting a Bentley with Honda money, and when does that ever happen? No shade to Honda, but it's facts. In your personal and professional life, people will stay tryna play you. They know how valuable you are, they're just hoping you don't. When someone tries to shortchange you, don't trip. Your worth is not up for debate. Bentleys don't get mad that you can't pay full price for them. Your inability doesn't depreciate their value.

Some of y'all missed that, but I'll run it back.

There are some people who will count the cost of your standards, your portfolio, or your expertise, and they will be unwilling or unable to pay the price for it. It doesn't change your worth. It just means they're not the right ones to receive the fullness of everything you have to offer. S'all good; the same thing happened to Jesus.

> They know how valuable you are, they're just hoping you don't.

Jesus was madd gassed to go back to Nazareth as a hometown hero. If people thought the miracles He performed everywhere else were lit, they weren't ready for what He'd been storing up for His day ones! Unfortunately, when He got home, they treated Him like a second-rate prophet, and discounted the heck out of His ministry. The whispers were loud and shady. *"Who he think he is? Ain't that the carpenter's boy? Gurrl, that ain't nobody but Jesus. I went to school with his sister. Didn't you change his diaper when he was a baby? So why he acting like he better than us now?"* You know it's bad when Da Good Book says that not even *Jesus* could perform any good works in that kind of environment.

Just because the Nazarenes couldn't receive His greatness, it didn't stop Jesus from actually *being* great. He didn't walk around saying, "Deng, I really thought I was the Messiah. I guess that's a wrap." Nope. He just kept it pushing, and that's exactly what you gotta do when folks try to downplay your magnificence. Maybe you've gone back home and the crew ain't what it used to be. Your friends disregard your achievements, and your family is madd skeptical about your life changes. Even your dog is looking at you sideways. Truth is, you've outgrown who you used to be, and that's something to be proud of, not ashamed about. The butterfly ain't tripping 'cuz it used to be a slimy, sluggish caterpillar. Both versions of you needed to exist in different seasons to get you to exactly where you are now. So spread your wings and fly, boo!

In Da Good Book, Caleb was that guy who wasn't interested in conforming to public opinion. He didn't care who was for him or against him, as long as God was with him.

> *Keep it pushing when folks try to downplay your magnificence.*

After escaping Pharaoh & Phriends, God promised to give the Israelites the land of Canaan, but there was one small hiccup: Someone else was already renting the spot. Joshua, Caleb, and ten other spies were sent to check out the competition and report back. Of the twelve spies, only Caleb and Joshua returned with a positive outlook. They believed that if God had already promised them the land, then what was there to discuss? The other ten spies weren't 'bout that life, though. They started spreading fear through the masses, telling them that the people in Canaan were like giants, and next to them, they felt like grasshoppers.

Grasshoppers y'all.

You've got God's chosen people, the same folks who He'd just rescued out of captivity, calling themselves not blessed, not victorious... but grasshoppers.

That's a no bueno.

How you view yourself determines how you'll allow others to see you as well. Because they saw themselves incorrectly, they never experienced the land that God had laid out for them. Forty-five years after the initial trip to Canaan, Joshua and a new crop of men with higher self-esteem were finally ready to take ownership of the Promised Land. But Caleb wasn't about to be left out a second time. At eighty-five years old, he told Joshua, "Don't let these gray hairs fool you. I ain't nobody's grasshopper, but I am here to get what's got my name on it, and I'll slapbox you and anybody else for it." Josh didn't want no smoke from an old, faith-filled man, so he gave Caleb everything he asked for.[1]

You are exactly who you think you are, even if it's a far cry from what God actually thinks of you. I wish you could see you the way the Heavens do. When I was getting bullied in middle school, my mom

---

1. See Joshua 14.

> You are exactly who you think you are, even if it's a far cry from what God actually thinks of you.

tried three different tactics to change my perspective on the situation. First, she attempted the typical Nigerian parent solution: **denial**. As far as she was concerned, this was a nonissue, because once again, she did not come to America for me to make friends, but to make straight A's. When the problem persisted, she switched to a softer approach: **deflection**. She told me not to worry about the girls making fun of me because they were all just jealous of me. As much as I wanted to believe her, I knew that wasn't true. They actually had friends who they sat with at lunch and shared Lunchables and Capri Suns, while I sat at the teachers' table. Backed into a wall, she had one more weapon left in the arsenal: **dominance**. She told me that if I kept working hard in school, then one day, I would eventually be their boss.

I was twelve years old and this woman already saw me having employees! And you know what? She wasn't wrong. Today I'm the CEO of my own company and I have a staff on payroll. But in eighth grade, telling those girls I was gonna be their boss only got me punched in the face. Somehow, like Caleb, I still managed to develop the tenacity to chase after the things I wanted and I wouldn't be persuaded otherwise. For instance, in high school, I was adamant that my first time having sex would include rose petals, candles, a waterbed, and satin sheets, all set to the tune of Maxwell's "This Woman's Work"—Don't judge me. *Love and Basketball* is still my favorite movie, remember.

All the girls at my school tried to crush my dreams by telling me that I'd be lucky if I got the back seat of some guy's car. The back seat of wh—? Have you *met me*? Even in ninth grade, I knew enough to know that wasn't gon'cut it. So I decided to wait for the guy who cared enough about me (and had the funds to afford a waterbed). With every passing year, I watched as I quickly became the lone member of the V-club. But I wasn't fazed. I was gonna get my satin sheets!

Although I'm still single and waiting, I haven't given up hope that Mr. Right will find me, but I have given up on the waterbed—I'll take a memory-foam mattress instead. Standards are yours alone to set. The same way Bentley manufacturers have determined the car's worth based on the German engineering, meticulous hand-stitching, and the European leather that goes into each creation, we, too, were designed in a Heavenly factory that's custom-built us for luxury performance. So go ahead and set that bar wherever you want. If people can't meet it, that doesn't mean it's too high. They just might be too short...

> We, too, were designed in a Heavenly factory that's custom-built us for luxury performance.

CHAPTER 19

GIVE GOD A BIG BAG TO FILL

Having a Nigerian mother, I'm well aware of the multipurpose function of a big bag. Those sturdy shoulder straps carry unlimited potential within their stitching. My mom didn't fool with clutches or those cute lil' purses. Nah. Those were just for show. When you have four children to feed at any given moment, you need a bag with girth. I remember when my brothers and I would go to the movies, we would beg Celine for popcorn, soda, and other treats from the concession. Each time she'd shut us down with the quickness, telling us she already got us food. We'd all exchange confused glances because we didn't remember seeing her standing in any lines.

When we were all settled in our seats and the previews began, that's when CeeCee would reach into her big ol' bag and pull out several Tupperware containers, each filled with jollof rice, jerk chicken, and plantains. She'd hand us our own containers, a plastic fork, and a napkin. Then she'd reach back into the bag to pull out a bottle of water,

Fanta, or a grape soda for us to make our selection. This woman had an entire picnic for five in that bag! As embarrassed as we might've been, the benefits of Momma's big bag were undeniable, and we profited greatly whenever she filled it up.

In the same way, God relishes the opportunity to fill the bags we give Him. Unfortunately, too many of us are bringing Him change purses and travel-size containers, as if we don't want to be a bother. We downplay our birthright and forfeit our inheritance when we act like we're Airbnb renters instead of joint heirs to the Kingdom. It all belongs to us. Somebody gotta get it, so why not you? Giving God a big bag to fill stretches our faith and expands our capacity to believe. I'll never forget telling God that I only wanted to make one payment to pay off my student loans. I didn't know how I was gon'do it as a struggling artist, but that was my bag, and I trusted Him to fill it. I deferred so long that GW almost asked for their diploma back, until one faithful day, it happened. I stacked up enough checks from *Insecure* and called Ms. Ruth at accounts payable to zero out my balance. I ended up overpaying and after all those years of owing *them*, they sent me a refund check. God got jokes!

In Da Good Book, there was yet another widow who was stuck in a stressful situation. Her husband had died and left her a rack'a debt to deal with. She didn't have the funds to settle with his creditors, so they took her two sons as collateral.

Y'all thought paying student loans was

> We downplay our birthright and forfeit our inheritance when we act like we're Airbnb renters instead of joint heirs to the Kingdom.

rough; these jokers were coming for her next of kin. The widow went to the prophet Elisha for help, explaining that the only thing she had of value was a small jar of olive oil. Elisha instructed her to hit up all her neighbors and grab every empty jar they had. He warned her not to try and act all bashful and only ask for a few. Nah, this wasn't the time for weak requests, not if she was serious about saving her sons.

Too often, pride keeps us from seeking help, but God uses people to deliver the answers we've been praying for. Those empty jars prolly didn't mean anything to her neighbors. They were about to be in the recycle bin. But to the widow, they represented the ransom for her sons. Once she'd gathered as many as she could, Elisha ordered her to fill the jars with the little oil she had left. As she poured, God supernaturally provided enough oil to fill every last one. Elisha then told her to head to the farmers' market to sell the oil and use the profits to pay off her debts. That would'a been amazing all by itself, but it didn't stop there. He said that she and her sons could live off what was left.

What was *left?!*

How many jars did they have? And what was the going rate for EVOO back then? That must've been Whole Foods prices. It blows my mind how God exceeded the widow's expectations. His supply met not only her immediate need, but the needs of future generations. That's what happens when you bring Him a large enough bag or, in her case, jar to fill.

You have not simply because you've asked not. Or maybe you're coming up short because of *how* you're asking. Whenever I get a DM or email message that starts with, *"You might never respond to this, but…"* I think to myself, *Deng, you canceled out yourself before you even got started, boo.* What's the point of putting yourself out there if you don't expect any good to come from it? That ain't faith; that's a leap of fear. Expectation is free. It costs nothing to believe that someone can and will go out of their way to make things pop off for you. Even if it doesn't happen, at least you had your expectors up. If I never do respond, it's because that person's words became a self-fulfilling prophecy. I was just filling their bag with exactly what they expected: nothing. If that's what folks are doing with me, imagine what they're doing with Jesus, and like mimosas, He's the one with a bottomless bag of resources.

Giving God a big bag to fill is like daring Him to be exactly who He said He would be. I love it 'cuz I get buck with Him, like He owes me something, kinda like how David came at Him when he needed a hookup from Heaven. He told God, "Lissen here, bruh, what good is it if I die? Will the dust praise You? Will it proclaim Your faithfulness? Nope. So it would be in Your best interest to help me. Thanks in advance."[1] David could only ask God for help, because he knew He was good for it. You don't ask your broke friends for gas money. They ain't got it. God's got streets paved with gold, so I'm sure He can let you hold a brick or two.

In the book of Malachi, God promised that when we give generously, He would open the windows of Heaven and pour out such a blessing that not even the Container Store could hold it. Challenge accepted. I hope Jesus got Venmo, Paypal, or Zelle, 'cuz I want mine direct deposited. Buying my first home was a perfect opportunity to give God a chance to make good on His promise. After years of renting, I was ready to own a piece of

> *Expectation is free. It costs nothing to believe.*

---

1. See Psalm 30:9–10.

the American Dream, but the LA real estate market wouldn't let me be great. My realtor, Ikem, and I searched for the perfect place but kept coming up short. If we found something I actually liked, I was beat out by buyers with all-cash offers.

The whole thing was bananas. When I didn't have money, I couldn't even think of getting a house. Now that I had the funds, I couldn't get anyone to take it. I clearly needed to have a heart-to-heart with Jesus. And by heart-to-heart, I mean I got right in His face and informed Him that had I kept my tithes and offerings, I would've had more than enough money to get into these overpriced homes. But I didn't keep it, I gave it, and I had the receipts! I'd helped to build the house of God, so now it was God's turn to help me get a house of my own. In hindsight, I think all those housing disappointments were God's way of saying, *"I'm still filling the bag. Don't settle."*

Finally, one sweet summer day, the unthinkable happened. Ikem sent me the listing for my dream house. We'll call it the house on Brier. It had everything: views, a pool, a firepit, a theater room. And it was in my desired neighborhood, with one of the best school districts. I was far from having anybody's baby, but that didn't matter. This house was looking out for my unborn kids.

I toured the home on four different occasions, brought friends with me, prayed over the grounds, laid hands on the walls, and even took pictures by the pool. You couldn't tell me I wasn't gonna be hosting barbeques and game nights on that property. Ikem didn't love Brier as much as I did, and I thought he was trippin'. Okay, yes, fine…there was a bit of a privacy issue. The house was sandwiched between three other homes that had direct views into my backyard and master bedroom.

But when you're in love, you don't see all the imperfections. You only see what the heart wants to see.

I tried to convince myself that it was a quick fix; nothing a few extra trees couldn't solve. *Right?* I put in my best and final offer and prayed for God's favour. But once again, my best just wasn't good enough. The seller wanted $100k more than I'd offered, and I was already *over* my budget. To make matters worse, I found out there was another couple putting in an offer, so if I wanted to secure this place, I had to pull the trigger fast. I talked to my financial team about my options, and while I could afford the asking price, they cautioned that with my budget already so stretched, I didn't want to be house rich but cash poor.

Ugh! Why was this so hard, Jesus?

The sellers ended up accepting the other offer, but I was ready for battle. I saw the "pending" status on Zillow and thought, *It ain't over 'til God says it's over. Anything can happen, and when this falls out of escrow, like Sir Mix-a-Lot, "I'll pull up quick to retrieve it!"*

But it didn't fall out of escrow.

The day I saw the status change from "pending" to "sold," I definitely shed a thug tear, like Denzel in the movie *Glory*. It felt like I'd just been bicycle-kicked in the throat. We'd looked at so many houses that I hated, and finally, the one that was nearly perfect just slipped through my fingers. By this time, it was August, and we'd started the search in March. I wanted to be settled into my house by December so I could celebrate my first Christmas as a new thirty-five-year-old homeowner.

It would've been one thing if I'd lost Brier in August and found the next-best thing a week later; heck, a month later. But nope. Month after month went by, and still nothing. This is probably where most of us would stop trusting the process and start believing that God isn't interested in our bag or is somehow unable to fill it. For you, it may not be a house. Your bag might be carrying a baby full-term or adopting the child that will make your family complete. Maybe your bag is a relationship. Your last one broke your heart, and they've since moved on, while you're still single on all the apps, wondering when it'll be your turn to catch a break. Work might be your bag. You know you're talented. You've got the qualifications, but you're still coming up short. Whatever your bag is, one thing's for sure: You need God to fill it to the max.

By November, I was done playing games. Habakkuk 2:2 tells us to write the vision and make it plain, so that's exactly what I did. I got madd specific and held nothing back. Even when my thoughts tried to tell me, *You don't need all'a that*, I told them to shut it up. This was my vision and I wasn't gonna limit God's hand. I even got downright indignant with Ikem, telling him that he had until Christmas to make something shake, and on November 3, I sent him this message:

YVONNE'S HOUSING WISH LIST— THIS IS THE BAG I'M GIVING GOD TO FILL

1. In my preferred zip codes and my comfort zone mortgage
2. Interest rate of 4.0 or better
3. Turn-key. No construction needed
4. Modern layout
5. Mix of open concept and defined spaces
6. Has a "WOW!" factor. Lots of nooks and crannies
7. 2,800 square feet and above
8. On a quiet and developed street

9. Private home (no view of neighbors) w/ greenery to provide tranquility
10. Ample parking spaces (not zoned)
11. Large wall for TV projector
12. Two separate living rooms
13. Big kitchen with 6-burner range and large island with barn sink
14. Stainless steel appliances
15. Light and airy w/ lots of natural light
16. White and gray tones or dark brown (but not that redwood!)
17. Wood accents/reclaimed wood/shiplap
18. Hardwood floors throughout
19. Sophisticated finishes
20. Fireplace and patio in main living room area
21. Large washer and dryer (not stacked)
22. 3-car garage
23. 3–4 fully renovated bedrooms w/ equal number of bathrooms
24. At least one half bath outside of bathrooms allocated to bedrooms
25. Large master w/ walk-in closet, fireplace, soaker tub w/ separate shower and water closet
26. Lights with dimmers
27. Heated floors
28. Separate office
29. Spacious areas for entertaining
30. Swimming pool or space to add one. Outside lounge area
31. No views of power cables

Whatever your bag is, one thing's for sure: You need God to fill it to the max.

32. Unobstructed views of the city
33. Friendly neighbors
34. A house that I will love and hands-down agree is MINE!

Ikem responded with, "CHALLENGE ACCEPTED!" so we went back at it with a vengeance. But the more we went out, the less we saw. As much as I tried to hold on to my bag, I started getting desperate, and when you get desperate, you make decisions from a place of panic, not peace. Before I knew it, I was looking at homes in areas I *knew* I didn't want to live in. We were now in December, and if you know anything about real estate, December is a very slow month for buying or selling. I turned thirty-five on December 2, and I truly had everything I wanted…except a house.

> When you get desperate, you make decisions from a place of panic, not peace.

On the sixth, Ikem gave me a very stern talking-to, and told me he wouldn't allow me to compromise on my vision. I'd made him a believer in the bag, and now, he was running full-speed with it, reminding *me* of the very thing I said I believed in! We all need people in our lives who will stir up our faith when we're teetering on the verge of giving up. So I surrendered to the process, for real this time. The next morning, I lie to you not, Ikem sent a listing with the following message: "THIS WON'T LAST." I flipped through the pictures, and with each swipe, my jaw kept dropping. What was the catch? Does it have asbestos? Is this real? Where did this come from? This house was right on budget, looked amazing, and was the first thing since Brier sold in August that had gotten me this excited! Could it be Jesus? *Could it actually be?*

Even though the first open house wasn't for another week, by the favour of God, the seller's realtor, K.T., allowed me to be the first one to see the house *that night*. When God's got a blessing with your name on it, it can't be denied. I walked through every room and couldn't believe how true to the pictures they were. I continued the tour, and when I sat in the garden, I felt such a peace from Heaven. Undoubtedly, I knew this was my home. Ikem drafted the offer that same night, and I made sure it included the number 7. Something in my spirit said that somebody associated with the home had an infatuation with that number. The house was listed on the seventh and the listing price had a 7 in it. It might have been nothing, or it might have been everything. Either way, I was picking up what they were putting down. I also wrote the sellers a personalized letter to include with my offer to drive home the sale.

Two days later, Ikem called to tell me they'd accepted my offer. I was beyond gecked! This was actually happening. When we went to sign the documents, K.T. told me that there was indeed another offer on the house at $200k above asking. However, the sellers really appreciated my letter. He also told me that it was a nice touch to add a "7" to the offer. The number held sentimental value to him, so he purposely added it to the listing. Jesus be knowin'!

After a grueling nine-month search, God gave me what didn't make any sense at all. Of the 34 items on my checklist, I got 32 of them. I said I wanted a tranquil outdoor space and I got 13,000-square-feet worth. I'd "lost" what I thought was my dream house, which was a solid $100k above budget, but ended up with a gem of a home at $100k below budget. When God shows up, He shows off *and* shows out! What have you "lost" that you thought was the best you would ever get, do, be, or have? It might've been good. There's no denying that. But baby, I got news for you. God is about to do something so dumb in your life, even your losses will congratulate you.

The blessings didn't end there. I'd gotten approved for a loan with a 4.25 percent interest rate. It wasn't the 4.0 percent or better that I'd hoped for, but my credit was still in repair, so I was ready to accept it. But God wasn't. Late in the midnight hour, on the day I was to sign closing documents, another bank swooped in and offered me a 4.0 percent rate. It's like God wouldn't let even me go against what I was believing Him for. He had my enormously big bag and intended on filling every aspect of it.

What bags make you nervous for God to fill? Which ones have you feeling unworthy of receiving His best? Go ahead and bring them anyway. Lay at His feet every outrageous thought. The ones that you try to self-edit and make more practical so they can be more attainable— bring those to Him in their rawest form. He won't set you up to settle. So, go ahead and put the Almighty to work. He doesn't do the bare minimum with our lives, He does the exceedingly, abundantly above and beyond. If you're gonna dream, you might as well go big, or go home, but not to my house.

> *God is about to do something so dumb in your life, even your losses will congratulate you.*

CHAPTER 20

Don't Put a Period Where God Put a Comma

I'm always curious about who the first person was to invent certain things and why. Like, who was the first person to put peanut butter on one slice of bread and jelly on another, and think to themselves, *These two should be joined together in holy sandwich matrimony*? Don't get me wrong, I'm glad they did it, but what was going on in their lives at that time to come up with such a concoction? When I looked up who invented carbonated water, I was shocked to learn that it was actually created by accident. Yup, the thing so many of us consume on a daily basis started out as a mistake. That's one lucrative mishap, if you ask me. God, I'mo need You to *stumble* me into some thangs.

There's just some things you can't predict. Like carbonated water, some of your wins might happen by trial and error. For the planners, I know you just had an anxiety attack. Deep breaths. There are some folks who spend every waking minute researching and information gathering, and what ends up happening is that they exhaust themselves and never get off dead center. Other people are so cerebral that they'll jump ten feet ahead to deduce all the reasons why something won't work. Don't put a period where God put a comma.

There's no formula for how things are *supposed* to go. When you're first starting out, it's likely that the joke will bomb. The audition will suck. The first draft will be wack. You'll lose the competition. The cake'll taste like chalk. The baby won't stop crying. The students won't care. The design will fail. You'll flunk the test. I say all of this not to discourage you, but to remind you that God created messy, flawed, petty you—and while He may let you fall, He'll never let you fail. So just relaaax. The only thing you're *supposed* to do is stay hydrated and keep growing.

Dassit.

Honestly, I couldn't have planned out my life if I tried. Nothing made sense. I started in entertainment at twenty-four—an age many people would consider to be late. I didn't get my first big break 'til I was thirty-one. While my friends had houses and kids, I had hopes and dreams. But if I had applied extreme logic to the process, I would've crippled my progress. Even now, in success, it feels like there's even more uncertainty. What will my next job be? Do I focus on movies or stick with TV? Should I branch out from comedy and tackle dramas? I'onkno! And that's part of the bamboozlement—to not know.

> God created messy, flawed, petty you—and while He may let you fall, He'll never let you fail.

I even got bamboozled into writing this book. While we were waiting to film the first season of *Insecure*, I guess God assumed I had nothing but time on my hands, so He asked me to dedicate one year to studying the Bible. In the process, I began making YouTube videos that were a snapshot of how I would interpret Bible stories through music, movies, and jokes. I called them my insperhumor productions, because I really wanted to fuse my love for Jesus with my love for '90s R&B.

I made a commitment to releasing a new video each month. I didn't have a big platform back then, so after pouring endless hours into editing, I'd only get a few hundred views. I thought to myself, *What's the point?* Then God asked, *"Are you doing this for the likes, or because I asked you to?"* Ooop. My bad.

The last video was uploaded in November 2016, and I got my book deal in November 2018. What I hadn't expected was that by creating that content, I was actually setting up the backdrop for what this book would become. By the time I sat down to write *Bamboozled* in 2019, I discovered that I already had several chapters mapped out. Thanks to those videos I didn't think anyone was watching, I got me a *New York Times* bestselling book that millions will read. (Hey, you gotta faith it 'til you make it!)

I couldn't have planned how my comedy tour and special would turn out either, but Jesus was all up in the mix, setting me up to be bamboozled one'mogain. If it were up to me, I would'a done my tour in the summer, when the weather is nice and hot. I hate everything about the cold. Once I left the East Coast, I was done with snow and winter weather advisories. (Un)fortunately, because of my filming schedule, the only window for me to do a national tour was from January to February 2020. Jesus had jokes, and I wasn't laughing.

I shot my special on February 29, and while I was so concerned about a snowstorm shutting us down, I didn't expect to be racing against the clock of an impending pandemic. Fourteen days later, errrythang got shut down thanks to corona. When I think about that moment, I marvel at how God *literally* gave me an extra day with a leap year to make my dreams come true.

Oh, but there's more.

Days before my special was set to premiere in June, the killing of George Floyd occurred, setting off national protests, with Black people demanding justice and for their lives to matter. The country was hurting and people were tired. The last thing I wanted to be was insensitive to the cause by promoting a special while people were dying in the streets. I prepared for the special to be a casualty of the times, and while it hurt personally, there was a larger moment being had.

One night, I got a message from a beautiful stranger that read, "*Hey Yvonne, I realize you're not able to promote your show as much because of what's happening in the world. I just want to assure you that your fans haven't forgotten, and we're waiting expectantly for your HBO special. Watch how Jesus will bamboozle you.*" All the thug in me left, as the tears started to flow. Who sent this woman and how did she know my innermost thoughts? If that ain't a kiss from Heaven telling me to rest assured, I don't know what is. I actually think the phrase "rest assured" makes more sense with a period separating the two words, so it reads, "Rest. Assured." Because if we truly believe God has infinite possibilities to get us to our destinies, then even in ambiguity, we could still rest, being fully assured that God's got us covered. It turned out that in the middle of a pandemic and racial tension, my comedy ended up being the relief and healing that audiences needed, if only for an hour.

The show went on to be one of the most watched specials on HBO that year.

That's the beauty of being bamboozled. In Da Good Book it says that the foolishness of God is wiser than all human wisdom.[1] That means that on your best day, you can't even begin to scratch the surface of what God's got up His sleeves. He made the sun stand still and the moon stop orbiting, just 'cuz one man needed extra time.[2] So you really think your fourth-quarter projections and "best-case scenarios" make a bit of a difference to Him? Not at all. Go ahead and loosen the reins a lil' bit and give God control. He's good for it. Call around and check His references. He's got a 7-star rating and specializes in the undeniable.

> Even in ambiguity, we can still rest, being fully assured that God's got us covered.

---

1. See 1 Corinthians 1:25.
2. See Joshua 10:13.

PART V

The Bonus

CHAPTER 21

CAN'T WEAR
A CROWN WITH
YOUR HEAD DOWN

Growing up, I was raised to believe that martyrdom was a way of life. No one explicitly said these words to me, but they exemplified it through their actions. If you weren't sacrificing yourself for the benefit of others, then what kind of Nigerian woman *were* you? I repeatedly watched the women in my life bend over backward (and sometimes break) to make it to a baby shower, cook for a birthday, give for a wedding, all in the name of "what will they say if I don't do it?" I wish I could say that I avoided falling into the same trap, but sadly, I, too, am down with OPP—occasional people-pleasing.

In the early stages of my career, I would jump on a bus from NY to DC every Friday and return on Sundays, just to please my parents. It defeated the entire point of my living in New York. I wasn't taking advantage of the weekend creative scene, and I was fooling myself by thinking I was making the situation at home better.

What I thought was a peace offering was actually a weekly declaration of war. Instead of my visits showing my parents that I still prioritized them, they were actually like scratching the scab off a freshly healed wound, reminding them of my failures as a daughter all over again. Finally, a cousin stepped in and made it clear that my folks wouldn't be happy unless I was either entering med school or marrying a doctor, so I might as well accept their disappointment and stay my butt in New York.

I was trying to be all things to everyone and becoming nothing to no one in the process. You can't serve two masters, but there I was, trying to accommodate both fear and faith, at the same darn time. Da Good Book warns against a double-minded mentality, suggesting that we be either hot or cold in our actions, 'cuz if we're lukewarm, that's when we get spit out. The *Message* translation is even more gangstarr with it. It says, "You're not cold, you're not hot…You're stale. You're stagnant. You make me want to vomit,"[1] PeriodT. As harsh as that sounds, I hope it's exactly what you need to hear to start choosing yourself today.

Self-sabotage isn't a badge of honor. It isn't a noble act to be celebrated. It's a slow, sad, unforgiving death of peace and joy. The world has made us feel bad for choosing ourselves, but it's time to teach our kids that "selfish" isn't a dirty word. Think about it—the only time it's socially acceptable to be a lil' selfish is literally when a plane is about to crash. That's when no one side-eyes you for doing as instructed and putting your oxygen mask on *first*, before thinking about your child, or the elderly lady next to you. That's ludicrous. The problem is, the wrong people have ruined the word "selfish." They linger in that space too long and suck out any compassion for humanity. That's not what

---

1. See Revelation 3:15–17.

I'm talking 'bout. I'm talking about the kind of selfish that forces you to ask some hard-hitting questions like, "What do I want? Does this make me happy? Why am I *really* doing that?"

I admit, I've never been good at being selfish. Between hustling to make it and working hard to maintain making it, I've always had to be the responsible one, the compassionate one, the selfless one. But I'm tih'd. Unlike Whitney Houston, I'm not every woman. It's not all in me. I thought that if I took care of other people, then surely, someone would return the favour, but that's not how any of this works. If you're always giving, people will always be taking. So it's up to you to set the appropriate boundaries.

Let's be honest, do you really want everyone to like you? Why? You don't even like everyone yourself. I aspire to Apostle Paul levels of unbothered when it came to pleasing people. In Galatians, he says, "As for those who were held in high esteem—whatever they were,

> *I was trying to be all things to everyone and becoming nothing to no one in the process.*

makes no difference to me," and posed the question, "Am I now trying to win the approval of human beings or of God?"[2] That's an important distinction for us to make ourselves. If your sole purpose is to win other people's approval, then be prepared to be limited by what their approval gets you.

The reality is, you trying to be relatable to the masses is actually preventing you from being relevant to your purpose. The goal isn't to

---

2. Galatians 1:10; 2:6 NIV.

be relatable; it's to be respected. There's a difference. Some folks fear getting too successful because people will say they've changed. Others are too afraid to try for their dreams, because if it doesn't work, people will call them a failure. Lemme help you out: Folks will talk about you whether you're doing good, bad, or nothing at all, so you might as well do what'chyu gonna do way big, and let'em deal with it. Shrinking yourself for the benefit of others is played out. We left that back in 2020, along with not washing your hands.

In Da Good Book, people-pleasing literally got Samson killed. He had good hair, which was the source of his superhuman strength. Before he was born, an angel told his momma that his locks could never be cut, faded, or edged up, lest he would lose all his power. Samson held that secret close to his chest, until he fell in love with Delilah. She pressed him to know why he was so skrong, and wanting to please her, he told her errrythang. That was his first and last mistake. Delilah turned around and snitched to the Philistines, Samson's worst enemies. Of course, when they found out his kryptonite, they cut the mess outta his hair, gouged out his eyes, and he died going down fighting.

When you place greater emphasis on how people perceive you, you choke the potential out what makes you, *you*. Proverbs says that your gift makes room for you. That means your talent creates avenues for you to reach greater heights. Utilizing your gifts, in your own authentic way, is what separates you from an overcrowded sea of more-of-the-same. It's easy to be swayed by what's popular and what's trending at the moment, but half the time, people don't know what they're hungry for until you Uber Eats it to their doorstep. That's why it's critical for you to stay true to what makes you indispensable.

When I started pitching the concept for *FirstGen*, I was adamant that it be a wholesome family show that different generations could enjoy together. After several meetings, I was still being asked, *"Is there any way to make it dirtier? A bit grittier?"* Then came the #MeToo, #TimesUp movements, along with a global pandemic forcing households to stay home, and suddenly the conversations shifted to, *"You know, what we love about the project is how pure and family friendly it is, which is exactly the kind of content we need in these dark times we're living in."* You'll never get the full benefit of doing you if you never actually *do* you. There's an old African proverb that says, *"If you think you're too small to make a big impact, try spending the night with a mosquito."* Your supply is necessary. What you have to offer is valuable, even if you don't get the validation you crave.

I can honestly say that this is a book that only I could write. I mean, who else you know that can weave their love of Jesus, DMX, and jollof rice seamlessly into a single sentence? Exactly. I ain't fit'na bend my style or my story to make it more palatable for anyone, and neither should you. It's gonna take practice to overcome your people-pleasing tendencies. At times it'll be hard, but so was third grade, and you got over that, didn't you? Okay then.

You can't wear a crown with your head down, and try'na do

> Folks will talk about you whether you're doing good, bad, or nothing at all, so you might as well do what'chyu gonna do way big, and let'em deal with it.

da most is leaving you with the least and is stripping you of your royalty. Like Maya Angelou said, your crown has already been bought and paid for. Cock that joint to the side, and rock it like only you can. Your presence shifts culture, your gift outlasts generations, and your authenticity can't be denied. Go'n and give the people what they want and they didn't know they needed—and that's YOU, boo.

> Try'na do da most is leaving you with the least and is stripping you of your royalty.

CHAPTER 22

YOUR HATERS GON'
BE YOUR ELEVATORS

The late, great Bishop Biggie Smalls profoundly summarized the plight of the successful when he said, "Mo' money, Mo' problems." You know you're doing something right if you're attracting opposition. The enemy ain't attacking anyone who doesn't have something valuable on their life. You only get left alone when you don't pose a threat. Matter'fact, the fact that you have people coming against you should serve as a barometer of your success. Congratulations. You've made it.

Whether you know it or not, there's someone who's not happy that you're winning. They can't stand the fact that you get to live out your dreams so loudly. You ain't done nothing to them. But, your only crime against humanity is that you dared to succeed. Defiantly, you believed that better was available and you actually went for it. The nerve of you. You gotta understand that your come up reminds folks of where they stopped short. It ignites animosity over where they currently are(n't) in their own lives. Or maybe they're just unhappy about anyone else succeeding who isn't them. Regardless of the reason, you can't let other people's insecurities stop you from celebrating the fruits of your labor. If folks wannabe jealous of your success, then they had better been jealous of your failures.

What I love about Da Good Book is that it knew the day would come when you'd have to deal with hateration, so it built in a foolproof plan to help you withstand the attacks: Do nothing, but everything you've been doing. Dassit. That's the strategy. God said *He* would fight your battles. *He* would restore the years that were stolen from you. What the enemy meant for your evil, *He* would turn it around for your good. Nowhere in there does it say that you have to sneak-diss or sub-tweet. Nah, you just keep doing you, as excellently as you've been doing, and eventually those who conspire against you will trip over themselves to bless you.

That's what happened to a widow in Da Good Book. She tried everything she could to get justice from a disgruntled judge, but whenever she approached his chambers, he snubbed the mess outta her. Ol'boi was hating hard for no reason, but the widow was relentless. She kept coming back with more resolve until finally the judge caved. He said, "I don't fear God or care what people think, yet because this widow keeps bothering me, I will see that she gets justice."[1] Like my Forever First Lady, Michelle Obama, said, when folks go low, we gotta stay going high.

We overcome the negativity by being the ones to maintain our composure, our integrity, and our posture of faith. I know you wanna take some cheap shots, but the battle ain't yours to fight. God's got it

1. Luke 18:5 NIV.

handled better than Olivia Pope. It's also important to note that not every critique classifies as hate. Folks could just prefer something other than what you're offering, and that's fine. You'll be able to distinguish when the line from critiquing to hating has been crossed.

I personally don't understand the need for hateration, especially when there's plenty of room for everybody to win. Unfortunately, everyone doesn't see it like that. Don't try and make sense of it. Just know that you're covered. Scripture says that no weapon formed against you would ever prosper, but it never said that the weapons wouldn't *form.* The attacks will come, but you've got a promise from Heaven that they won't, in any way, shape, or form, succeed at bringing you down.

God takes it a step further and says that the same people plotting and scheming against you will eventually become your footstool. What's a footstool? Something you use to go higher. Basically, your haters are about to become your elevators. Can we stop for a sec and give Jesus a shout-out for the people in our lives who thought they were tearing us down, but ended up building us up. Hallelu!

There's a story in Da Good Book about a blind beggar named Bartimaeus who could co-sign that praise. He heard that Jesus was passing through, and he wanted more than anything to be able to see again. So he defied "normal protocol" and shouted loudly to get Jesus' attention. The entourage around Jesus thought Bartimaeus' tactics were too uncouth, so they told him to pipe down. But you know what Bartimaeus did? Shouted louder. And you know what happened

> If folks wannabe jealous of your success, then they had better been jealous of your failures.

next? Jesus told the crowd to bring Bartimaeus to Him. The same folks who'd just told the blind man to shut up were now the ones helping him to get up! You betta receive that testimony for yourself. The same folks who fix their mouth to downplay your shine will be the ones God uses to prop you up.

Folks love to box you into their way of thinking, acting, or even believing, so *they* can feel comfortable. Once they've categorized your future, then they can pigeonhole your experiences. Well, they can miss me with all that, because God didn't design you or me to conform. He made us to stand out. I had a friend who'd grown accustomed to me being the "struggling artist" in the group. Our friendship made sense as long as she held financial advantage over me. It was cute for me to have hope, and it was safe for her to believe in my dreams, so long as all I got were little sparks of success. But when my life exploded, all of a sudden the narrative became that I had changed. Aren't we supposed to? Since when was the goal to stay exactly the same?

I knew what she meant, though. At my core, I was still the same person she'd befriended, but the role she desired to play in my life no longer existed, so that was the end of us. Now, I don't condone leaving anyone behind, all willy nilly. But I will lap you in a heartbeat if you thought for five seconds that I would play small to placate your inadequacies. Good-bye and God bless. I'm certain a few folks in the crowd had grown accustomed to Bartimaeus, "the blind beggar," and couldn't process the change in status when Jesus restored his sight. How did *he* get to be healed when they were the ones who'd been grinding longer and praying harder for their own miracle? As salty as the haters might be, they don't get to write the rules for your success, and you ain't gotta get sucked into their vortex. The two places we' not going anymore are

(1) back and (2) forth. If you know that their attacks serve to take you higher, then, though they slay you, your hope remains in God, your defender.

You might not realize it, but some of your opponents might be hiding in plain sight—posing as frenemies or family. God knew that the biggest detractors to your purpose could very well share your last name, but He didn't leave you helpless. He covered you in the Word, baby. When your parents think you've lost it, Psalms reassures that, even if your mother and father abandon you, the Lord will hold you close. If your siblings suddenly stop rocking with you, Proverbs offers hope in a friend that sticks closer than a brother.

> The same folks who fix their mouth to downplay your shine will be the ones God uses to prop you up.

I certainly had my fair share of well-meaning family members who hated on my dreams in the in-between stages. There was the uncle who never missed an opportunity to remind me that I had two degrees I was wasting. His brilliant advice: Choose one to do something with. Then there was the aunt who occasionally sent job postings. I guess for her, the gold standard was to get a "good guv'ment job, with benefits." When these tactics failed, they sent in reinforcements. I started receiving random phone calls from perfect strangers, letting me know that "it wasn't too late to do something with my life." Of course, now that I've succeeded, these same family members lead the charge of sharing articles in group chats and bragging about their famous niece. It's all love, but it sure sounds like footstooling behavior to me.

When the negative voices are too loud to ignore, you can regain control and protect your mental health by clearing out the things that don't serve you. That could mean deleting every voice mail, blocking every tweet, DM, or text, that tries to paint a different picture of your future. Now, if you're the one with hating tendencies, then you've got some clearing out to do as well. Those thoughts that make you feel inferior gotta be canceled, and those accounts that leave you jealous gotta get unfollowed. You don't want to voluntarily make *yourself* somebody else's footstool just because you're envious. They'll end up stepping all over you as they continue their climb to the top.

Winston Churchill famously said that if you have enemies, that means you stood up for something, sometime in your life. Continue standing up in faith. Your story doesn't end in defeat. Folks can talk about you. They can smear your character, sabotage your efforts, even cancel you online, but they can never cancel God's plans. He'll raise you up higher and give you double for all your trouble.

> They can cancel you online, but they can never cancel God's plans.

CHAPTER 23

HERE WE GROW AGAIN

During the 2008 election cycle, there was a huge push to get young voters out. One particular message that stood out came from Diddy's Citizen Change organization. The famed mogul wore a T-shirt that read "VOTE OR DIE," and that became a symbol for highlighting what was at stake if we failed to invoke our civic duty.

I think a shirt that says "GROW OR DIE" could be equally effective in highlighting what's at stake if we refuse to mature into our best selves. Anything not growing is dying. Those are the only two options.

It's impossible to make strides into our future while we're still stuck in our past. Just ask Moses. He'd grown accustomed to one way of leadership. He was the one who spoke to God directly on the people's behalf, and relayed the message to the masses. While that might've been an effective communication strategy when the Israelites were on the run and needed a singular voice to guide them, it wasn't sustainable once they were all in one place and the demands from the people grew.

Moses became increasingly overwhelmed. Fearing a burn-out, his father-in-law, Jethro, advised him to appoint competent leaders who could share the responsibility of handling routine tasks and only bringing him the hard cases.[1] Basically, Jethro was teaching Moses the very necessary skill of delegation. Could God, or the Jethroes in your life, be requiring similar behavioral or structural changes from you in order to improve your overall performance? It's not profitable to you, your relationships, or your business to stay rigid in the old way of doing things. God is calling you higher.

Anything not growing is dying.

In Isaiah, God said plainly, "Forget the former things; do not dwell on the past. See, I am doing a new thing!… Do you not perceive it?"[2] Don't miss the new thing God is trying to do in you 'cuz you're stuck on the last thing He did through you. Growth is pertinent to success. You've never been this version of yourself before, and the new you requires new prayers, new partnerships, and new thought patterns to sustain your grind.

Like Moses, the things that worked to get you this far might only get you this far. And just 'cuz God tolerated a habit in one season, doesn't mean He'll let it slide in another. That was just His grace covering your weaknesses the whole time. Not because they weren't a problem, but because you didn't have the capacity to address them then. Don't be fooled into believing your shortcomings are actually your

---

1. Exodus 18:17–23.
2. Isaiah 43:18–19 NIV.

superpower. I'll never forget when my therapist told me that I was in denial. I scoffed at the remark. Me? A *whole* me, in denial? Impossible. That's what everyone else in my family is. I see clearly. Almost *too* clearly even. Dr. Robinson waited for me to finish and said, "Would you like me to use another word that means the same thing?" Ooop.

Personally, I never want to be in denial about the state of my affairs spiritually, emotionally, or mentally, so I had to attack the root of my issues head-on. Unfortunately, a lot of people seem satisfied with settling for the same'ol tired explanation of, *"That's just me."* They damage their futures with their tongues by saying things like, "I know I have anger issues, but that's just me." "I know I'm being petty, but that's just me." Pastor Mike would often ask, "Who is the person you call 'me,' and what are you allowing 'them' to keep you from?" Too many of us are wearing "me" as a badge of honor when it's really a rallying cry for change.

If you're the lowest common denominator in all your problems, it would be in your best interest to dig deep and get to the root of every issue that's tripping you up. Sure, it's difficult to digest the unflattering things we uncover about ourselves, but if I gotta live with me every day and my trash stinks, I'd rather change the bag than cover the stench up with Febreze. Everywhere you go, you take you along. So how is "you" doing?

If we're keepin' it real, change is hard. And the hardest part isn't even realizing you have to change. It's knowing you need to, but not knowing *how* to. It

> Too many of us are wearing "me" as a badge of honor when it's really a rallying cry for change.

takes work to achieve meaningful growth in our lives, but don't let that keep you complacent in your deficiencies. The author Wayne Dyer said that our lives are a sum total of the choices we've made. What's your life adding up to?

Every day Jesus gives us a choice. He says, "I set before you life and death, blessings and curses."[3] And in the same breath, He offers us a cheat code by telling us to "choose life." Sadly, not everyone alive is living and not everyone living is thriving. Far too many of us are merely existing. Now, I'm no expert in the field of growth studies, but through my experiences, I've noticed four traits in particular that keep a lotta people from living their best selves. This by no means is a comprehensive list, but they are the most common.

The first trait is **the stagnation of validation**. This is when people need someone to validate their existence, their ideas, or achievements through positive affirmation. Without it, they feel stuck in place and second-guess their ability to make a move—*any* move. Obviously, that's a rather risky gamble, because what if that endorsement never comes?

When I was a brand-new comic in DC, I got a message that a local manager, Charles Kane, had caught my performance and wanted to speak with me. I was pressed to hear if he thought I was any good. I needed to hear praise to substantiate my efforts. But Charles told me something that's stuck with me all these years. He said, "If you weren't any good, I wouldn't have gone through the trouble of getting your number. I'm not here to talk about what you did right. You already did that right. I'm here to tell you what you can do better."

My ego wanted him to acknowledge how hard I'd worked on the

---

3. Deuteronomy 30:19 NIV.

set. My pride wanted to ask what made him laugh the hardest. But Charles got me to look at success through an understanding that if I was having certain conversations with certain individuals, then I was *already* doing something right. All I needed to do was to keep fine-tuning what was innately in me. Lissen, I'm not tryna tell you that your love language being words of affirmation isn't important—it is. But not receiving them shouldn't torpedo your goals.

One of my favorite scenes from the movie *Love and Basketball* is when the lead character, Monica, shoots a beautiful jump shot. The ball goes in, and she stops to admire her handiwork. Meanwhile, the player she was supposed to be guarding scores at the other end. She was too busy gloating about the last thing she did right to notice the one thing she was doing wrong. As punishment, her coach sidelines her. Later in the movie, that same coach promotes her to a starting position, which baffles Monica. That's when the coach says, "You think I'd go hoarse for a player with no potential? When I ignore you, then you worry." Essentially, she was telling Monica that she recognized her skills, but also recognized her potential for growth. What felt like her riding Monica hard was actually the coach investing in Monica's future.

Internationally renowned speaker Jay Shetty once said, "If you let compliments get to your head, then you'll let criticism get to your heart." If you give

> If you give people the power to dictate your progress through their praise, then you're also giving them the power to fortune-tell your failures through their disapproval.

233

people the power to dictate your progress through their praise, then you're also giving them the power to fortune-tell your failures through their disapproval. Why should anyone have that much power over you? Even Jesus said, "My sheep hear my voice, and I know them. / A stranger will they not follow...for they know not the voice of strangers."[4] Get to know God's voice for yourself and focus instead on what He tells you about you.

You be your own hype-(wo)man. Take a moment to celebrate yourself. Do *you* think you did a good job? Great, keep doing more of that. Can *you* identify any areas of improvement? Wonderful, now dispatch the appropriate resources to make those changes. Do *you* believe your efforts were sufficient? Turn up then, and pat yourself on the back.

The second hindrance to growth is **the asinine of the co-sign**. It's first cousins with the stagnation of validation because they both deal with other people's approval affecting our ability to prosper. The difference is, those who suffer from the stagnation of validation are uncertain of their strengths. On the flip side, the folks who luxuriate in the asinine of the co-sign believe they are almost always right. They thrive when someone co-signs their point of view. As a result, they're only interested in recruiting people who side with them into their inner circle.

While they seek out opportunities for growth, it has to benefit their ideologies. The minute something challenges their preconceived notions, they immediately buck at it. I briefly dated a guy like this. Clearly, it didn't work out. He had a difficult time accepting certain aspects of my profession, so he sought counsel from his pastor. Expecting the man of God to co-sign his concerns, he was in for a shock

---

4. John 10:27, 10:4–5 KJV.

when he heard the pastor say, "Bruh, before she was ever your girl, she was God's daughter first. So if He's cool with it, who are you to have a problem with it?"

Where was the lie? I searched all over, still couldn't find it.

He thought he was gonna get co-signed but was big madd when he got counseled instead. That's the problem. A lot of people say they're open to change, but in reality, what they want is for someone to sign off on the exact make and model they are, with no upgrades. Sure, it's an ego boost to surround yourself with nothing but "yes" people, but very rarely does that lead to optimal growth. We have to allow God, and the right individuals, permission to prune us just like David did when he said, "Investigate my life, O God; find out everything about me; cross-examine and test me; get a clear picture of what I'm about; see for yourself whether I've done anything wrong—then guide me on the road to eternal life."[5] You can get co-signed, counseled, or corrected, *or* you can allow God to cross-examine you.

The third trait is **the blatancy of complacency**. The folks who fall into this category love inspiration, but loathe revelation. Inspiration takes copious notes, buys planners, listens to podcasts, makes vision boards, but at the end of the year, the vision is still foggy. This group likes the *idea* of change, but the *practice* of it, not so much. There's an entire line of sportswear called "athleisure" that's dedicated to people who are inspired by fitness and want to *look* like they work out, but really, they just want to be "out" without the "work."

---

5. Psalm 139:23–24 MSG.

> You can get co-signed, counseled, or corrected, or you can allow God to cross-examine you.

I've said this before, and I'll say it again—don't you dare just be "inspired" by my book. You gotta GO. You gotta DO. You gotta MOVE FORWARD! Putting action behind your inspiration, that's revelation. Once something has been revealed to you, it's impossible to pretend it away. You've seen too much, so now you gotta deal with it. These chapters should be a call to action—a springboard that propels you into being your best self.

The fourth and final hindrance to growth is **the possessing of the blessing**. This is an area I've personally struggled with. I'm sure you're thinking, *Hol'up, if you obtain the thing you've worked so hard for, shouldn't that inspire you to grow more?* In theory, yes, but sometimes the blessing can also become a burden. A lot of things have come at me fast, and it's been difficult to make the necessary transitions at times.

After gaining success with *Insecure*, I still possessed a poverty mindset. I'd gone without for so long that I was still in conservation mode. As "quickly" as my own Promised Land came after seven years in the wilderness, I didn't know if it would disappear at the same rate. So, I was chokeholding my blessings for fear of losing them. I had to remind myself of a lot of the same principles I'm sharing with you. That doesn't mean it was easy to get used to.

I'll never forget when I needed to hire an assistant, and my friend April encouraged me to spend a chunk of my first endorsement deal on their salary. That amount sounded ludicrous to give to one person, especially when I was just starting to stack coins. But being a business-woman herself, April helped me prepare a cost-benefit analysis. Ultimately, she convinced me that I would actually make *more* money that year if I invested into someone who could free me up to be more creative.

It's so critical to keep people around you who will save you from yourself and challenge you in your growth. Scripture says that iron sharpens iron, and while it may be uncomfortable at first, it's a lot better than staying dull. In the moments when I'm tempted to slip back into my old way of thinking, I remind myself to "light the candle." In the past, I would wait for special occasions to light really expensive candles I received as gifts. But what constitutes a special occasion to burn scented wax? Don't make things so precious that you don't enjoy them. So often we forget to live. We tell ourselves, "When I get married, then I'll buy a house. When I lose weight, then I'll go on vacation." Baby, treat yo'self tuh-day. Self-care isn't just massages and facials—it's feeding your soul and finding your joy. So be good to you. Pull the trigger on what satisfies and discover what edifies—that's growth.

Treat yo'self tuh-day! You've earned it.

CHAPTER 24

BEYOND THE BAMBOOZLEMENT

Like a Boyz II Men song, we've come to the end of the road. I hope that means that you've been peer-pressured into being *bamboozled by Jesus*. If so, congratulations. Maybe you've even taken it a step further and gotten tricked into the life of your dreams. Welcome. Does it feel like it was worth it? It should. Everything you've been through was divinely orchestrated to get you to this moment, and to prepare you for your next stop.

Oh, what, you thought you were done?

That's cute. But, nah, you're just getting started. You still have to live in the aftermath of your bamboozlement. That means getting acclimated with the joy and responsibility of the blessing. So before we part ways, I wanted to leave you with two final nuggets that have helped me maintain peace, stability, and a sense of self in the midst of the overflow.

The number one question I get asked is, "What advice would you give to someone considering a career in entertainment?" My answer is the same as I would give to anyone in any career, and that is to simply be a good human—that's a quality that never goes out of style. It means being a person of your word, treating others fairly, being honest and kind—you know, the basics.

It's amazing how far a handwritten card, mailed with a stamp (ask your parents what that is), or a delivery of flowers can go in saying thank you. If I have a meeting with someone and they tell me they have a major life event approaching, like running a marathon, I'll put it on my calendar, and when the date comes, I shoot them a text, an email, or, depending on the relationship, send them a care package, to encourage them on their big day. I make this a habit even with friends. If they're moving, I'll set an alarm to remind myself to check in on their progress. It's those little touches that set you apart and have a huge impact in your relationships.

Being considerate may not cost anything, but it sure does pay off. Da Good Book suggests that the memory of the righteous is a sweet-smelling aroma. Everywhere you go, you should give off a fragrance that points people to the goodness of God—and I'm not talkin' what perfume you're wearing. When I leave a room, I want an aura of joy to permeate the atmosphere. What lingers in the air after *you* exit? Is it a fragrance of gratitude or is it one of bitterness? You get to decide, and if it's the latter, you can always course correct.

Someone once told me that when a woman looks at you, it's for two reasons: Either she's admiring you, or she's jealous of you. Well, that just didn't sit right with me at all. If I'm checking you out, you better know it's 'cuz something about you is bomb. To remove any doubt, I make it a point to compliment at least one person a day. I stop women and tell them how beautiful they look or how dope their shoes are. I'm quick to tell a guy his beard-game is on point. You can most certainly acknowledge someone else's brilliance without diminishing your shine.

You never know how a kind word spoken to a stranger could impact both of your lives, like it did the day I met Jessica. I had just finished a speaking engagement and was racing out the building to head to the airport. While I waited for the car, a beautiful young lady with a short blond pixie cut walked past me, and I shouted out, "I love your haircut. It looks stunning on you." She turned around and self-consciously asked, "Do you really think so?" I gave her another compliment, and that's when she dropped the bomb on me: She had just been diagnosed with cancer and was about to start chemo. The haircut was for her to get used to the length before it eventually fell out.

> You can most certainly acknowledge someone else's brilliance without diminishing your shine.

I don't remember when the tears started falling, but they came in hot. I may not have had a cure for Jess, but I did have a strong, sincere hug in me. I held her close and told her she was stronger than she knew and prayed with her right there on the sidewalk. Every so often I wonder how she's doing and if she's kicked cancer in the butt yet. But one thing I don't ever have to wonder about is if I did my part in making her feel seen or valued in her time of need.

You never know who might *literally* be dying to hear something nice today. So I'm officially starting the #GiveOneGetOne challenge. I dare you to go out of your way to compliment at least one person a day for the next month. It could be the essential worker on duty or the mom who looks stressed the heck out on the Zoom call. Try to find something you genuinely like about them and acknowledge it. It's that simple.

No matter how much time and money you invest into improving your talent, if your attitude is trash, then so is your potential for success. Jay-Z said it best: "You can pay for school, but you can't buy class." I'm sure you know talented people whose personalities hold them back. I certainly do. In his book *Talent Is Never Enough*, John C. Maxwell writes that some incredibly gifted people coast on their abilities, in the hopes that their personal deficiencies will be overlooked. Hate to break it to you, but that setup doesn't have a long shelf life. Instead, every morning, while you're busting out your favorite essential oils, try dabbing on a splash of courtesy, care, and respect. The same rules apply: A little goes a long way.

The second nugget I'll leave you with is that being rich with a side order of sorrow is still poverty. If you don't believe me, ask Judas just how happy securing the bag left him. I'll spare you the Google search, it didn't. At the time, though, he thought it was a good idea to backstab his BFF Jesus in exchange for thirty silver coins. When he realized he'd made a terrible mistake, it was too late. Jesus was already sent to be crucified. The thing he did to get rich quick made him poor in spirit and in life.

I've seen firsthand how success has derailed a few folks, and it ain't pretty.

> No matter how much time and money you invest into improving your talent, if your attitude is trash, then so is your potential for success.

It's no bueno to be thriving outwardly, but lack peace internally. In Proverbs, it says that the blessings of the Lord make us rich and He adds no sorrow to it. It's definitely not the will of God to finally give you everything you've been praying for, only for those things to leave you void of contentment and satisfaction. That's what Pastor Steven calls "SUCKcess," and that ain't sexy.

A few months ago, I received a text that completely threw me for a loop. The individual who sent it is very successful—a brilliant performer, absolutely stunning, and by all accounts living the dream, which is why I was so baffled by the message. They shared that they'd been intentionally distancing themselves from me, and not 'cuz of the coronavirus. Apparently, despite their success, they still felt marginalized in the industry, and envied how I'd been embraced by it.

It's no bueno to be thriving outwardly, but lack peace internally.

I was shocked because I never would've imagined that this individual would carry such a perspective. I saw them as a complete and total boss, killing the game and taking names. Unable to make sense of it, I confided in a close friend to get her perspective on the situation. I told her that the individual who'd texted me had a larger social media following than me, and a much lengthier career. That's when my friend asked, "But are they happy?"

That's a question to ask yourself often. We're the only ones who can define what happiness means for us. After I hit a nice stride in my career, I found myself in this weird place where I was getting everything I'd worked so hard for, but something still felt empty. I had placed unrealistic expectations on what would happen once I finally "made it," and once those things didn't happen, I felt let down by life. I don't know why I'd expected that my family would suddenly understand what I did for a living, or that they'd appreciate all the sacrifices I'd made over the years to get to where I was, but I did.

When my pivotal moments came, even though they were celebrated with support, it didn't *feel* like how I imagined it would. When blessings make you rich in your accounts, but not in your soul, you gotta check the source. If they come with a dose of guilt, pain, or compromise, it might be the devil tryna throw you a counterfeit blessing, or it might actually be God's doing, but for some reason you can't receive it. Niecy Nash always says that the devil can't stop you from being blessed, but he can alter whether or not you enjoy the experience.

God was doing His part and pouring out blessings, but the devil was also doing his part and altering my joy in it. The fact is, my parents *were* very proud, but my world is foreign to them. They can only appreciate it on a level that makes sense to them. So no, they wouldn't suddenly know the names and relevance of the dope celebrities I was starting to work with, but they would watch all of my interviews on YouTube, and share them accordingly. Once I realized that my feelings were robbing me of my happiness, I decided to love my family exactly where they were at, not where I wanted them to be. This is your moment. These are your blessings. Jesus bamboozled you into them; don't let the devil trick you out of them.

> This is your moment. These are your blessings. Jesus bamboozled you into them; don't let the devil trick you out of them.

Well, there you have it. We're done for real, for real. Hopefully you've enjoyed reading about my journey as much as I've enjoyed reliving it. Maybe something in my life has enticed you enough to say, "I'll have what she's having," kinda like you would at a restaurant when you can't decide what to order. You look over to the table next to you and see how much they're enjoying their meal, and that settles it for you. No need to look further at the menu. The good news is that God is our Master Chef, and as long as you stay hungered for Him, your future will never be famished.

One of the best compliments I've ever received came from a young woman who said, "You make me want to be me when I grow up," and I loved it! Your life should also inspire others to wanna get in on it, too. I hope being *bamboozled by Jesus* is everything you never imagined it would be, and it makes you everything you always believed you could be. I don't know your name, I don't know your struggles, but I do know that you are necessary and your supply is abundant, and personally, I can't wait to be a benefactor of your bamboozlement.

"You make me want to be me when I grow up."

BAMBOOZLED BELIEFS

I love a good morning mantra, so here are a few of my faves to get your day started. Feel free to say them all at once, or once a day. It's your world. Go be great!

1. I believe I am above always and never beneath.
2. I believe all things work together for my good.
3. I believe God has gone before me making every crooked path straight.
4. I believe that when I seek God first, He causes everything else to be added unto me.
5. I believe favour follows me everywhere I go.
6. I believe somebody, somewhere is using their power, ability, and influence on my behalf.
7. I believe my name is being spoken favorably in rooms my feet have yet to enter.
8. I believe I will not lose. I cannot lose. I don't know how to lose.
9. I believe that if God gave the vision, He will bring the provision.

10. I believe I am enough, regardless of my qualifications, because God has qualified me.

11. I believe that no harm, hurt, or danger will come near me, my family, or my purpose.

12. I believe wisdom directs my steps and enables me to get out of the boat when needed.

13. I believe I'm a person of my word, and integrity protects me.

14. I believe God fills me with great ideas, and there is room for me in the marketplace.

15. I believe I deserve God's best, and I don't have to compromise my core values to get it.

16. I believe that I only have to outlast my darkest night by one day.

17. I believe that the lies of doubt have to bow down to the Truth of God's Word.

18. I believe I have high self-esteem because God esteems me highly.

19. I believe that no one else can be me, so I will stop discounting my greatness.

20. I believe that I will not be shaken, removed, or disqualified from my destiny.

21. I believe that my flaws keep my faith fine-tuned.

22. I believe that I'm not set in my ways, but I am set apart.

23. I believe that I am significant, necessary, vital, and wanted.

24. I believe I'm an asset to my community, and anyone who comes in contact with me is instantly blessed.

25. I believe I will excel at everything I set my mind to, and everything I touch will prosper.

26. I believe I walk in the boldness and authority that God has given me.
27. I believe that nothing and no one can stop the plans of God for my life, including me.
28. I believe I will show up as my highest self every single day.
29. I believe that God will expose quickly, reveal suddenly, and remove swiftly anyone who does not have my best interest at heart.
30. I believe I will find joy in my success.
31. I believe I will allow myself to get *bamboozled by Jesus!*

Acknowledgments

To Rita Sinha Marsh, Tiffany Green, and Ty Watts—Thank you for being incredibly generous with your time and reading through many ROUGH versions of this book and offering insightful, honest feedback. Iron sharpens iron and you three certainly made sure there was nothing dull about this book. I am beyond grateful.

To Pastors Mike and DeeDee Freeman, Lindsay Marsh Warren, and Tameshiah Shipley—Thank you for providing an outstanding foundation of faith. You showed me that it *was* possible to love God wholeheartedly, maintain your swagger, and live life abundantly. We ain't gotta choose. He's big enough to give us a purpose and also outdo Himself in fulfilling it.

To Pastor Steven Furtick and Bishop Jakes—Thank you for building upon the foundation that was laid. Your ministries have been food to my soul and sustained me in countless seasons.

To Luvvie, Boz, and Justina—My Sistahs of Life. You are the illest hype-squad anyone could ask for. Thank you for the klutch advice and the many ways you celebrate me.

To Issa—Thank you for remembering me at a time when I felt so forgotten. Your vision changed my life, and your friendship nourishes it.

To the Roommate Extraordinaire, Ester Lou—Thank you for enduring my many gripe sessions, for cheering me on with each edit completed, and being honest enough to give me the unpopular feedback.

To Daisy Hutton—my editor and publisher, THANK YOU. You saved my baby and saw the same beauty in her that I did. You pushed me beyond my comfort zone and challenged me to dig deeper. You allowed me space to be a creative and to not conform. I am grateful.

To DC, Brandi, Sam, Loan, Nina, and the entire Y.O. Team—Thanks for being 'bout it when it comes to supporting the vision and pushing it forward.

To the Glam Squad: Drini, Mary, and Apuje—Y'all kilt this cover shoot. **Allen Cooley**, you're vicious with the lens. I wrote the vision and you ran with it. Thanks, **Myleik**, for the intro! Thank you, **Alyssa Banks** for ALWAYS being ready for one of my design projects and **James Anthony**, you know we got plenty more collabos in us.

To my family: Afam, Ikem, Uche, Tope, Adagu, Iduu & Lolo—Your prayers ring Jesus' doorbell. I'm convinced of it. Also, thank you for the endless forwarded Whatsapp messages on the family group chat. Because, why not?

To everyone along this journey who was used mightily by God—whether it was long talks on a hike, late-night writing sessions, four-minute voice notes, Marco Polos, a couch to crash on, a prayer offered, consistent text check-ins, an internship, a gig, cash transfers to cover bills, or a hot meal when I took the term "starving artist" quite literally. There are too many of you to name, but you certainly know who you are, and I'm certainly grateful for all you've done.

To God, Jesus & Holy Spirit—Thank You for how You love me. Thank You for all You saw in me before I could see it in myself. Thank You for Your patience as I catch up to the version of me You always intended for me to be.

About the Author

Yvonne Orji is an Emmy-nominated Nigerian American actress, writer, and comedian. A failed doctor (blame organic chemistry), Yvonne took to comedy after needing a talent for a beauty pageant. Now she entertains international audiences, as can be seen in her one-hour HBO comedy special, *Momma, I Made It!* A sought-after speaker, she has given the opening keynote at the Forbes Under 30 Summit, and her TEDx talk, "The Wait Is Sexy," has garnered over a million views. Her breakout TV role was playing Molly on HBO's hit show *Insecure*. She currently resides in Los Angeles.